# When the Dinner Bell Rings at the Governor's Mansion

## Treasured Recipes Past and Present

# Table of Contents

# Dedication

Dedicated to my husband, Governor
Bob Riley, my greatest supporter.
Thank you for always believing in me.
I love you always.

# In Appreciation

With heartfelt gratitude,
I want to thank Peggy Collins, Leah
Dean, Alley Jackson, Hollon
McKay, Lee Sentell, Amy Shell,
Sherrie Stanyard and Lucile Waller
for all the hard work and
encouragement it took to help make
this cookbook a reality and for giving
of their time and talents to
our great state of Alabama.

I want to express my thanks to
Lee Sentell for all the extra help he
gave to me during the months
I've worked on this project.

Lee, I could not have completed this
cookbook without you.

# Introduction

In 1950, 1142 South Perry Street became the address for the Governor's Mansion of Alabama. Governor Gordon Persons and Mrs. Alice were the first to live in the mansion and every governor since has lived in the private quarters located upstairs. Five large, stately rooms and grounds are open to the public on Tuesdays and Thursdays by appointment.

When your spouse decides to run for governor and seek the highest office in your state, you run also. Even though you think you know what is involved in being a first lady or first gentleman, your job comes with its own set of responsibilities. So many wonderful opportunities have been added to my life as First Lady. I am deeply grateful, but the opportunity that gives me continued pleasure is opening the mansion doors to the public!

When the dinner bell rings at our mansion, it means great food, treasured memories of fellowship with family and friends, wonderful traditional recipes to be enjoyed at the meal and of course, recipes to share! Whether our mansion dining table is in a beach cottage, a lake cabin, a city apartment, a country farmhouse, a mountain chateau or a governor's mansion, when the dinner bell rings, it brings people we love together.

For all of us, our homes are our mansions and our food is more than ingredients to fill our bodies. Food brings pleasure after a busy day. Food brings rest after many difficult decisions have been made. Food brings comfort when words are hard to say. Food was created by God to give us strong bodies and minds. It gives us the energy and strength to do what He has called us to do in this life.

When the dinner bell rings at the Alabama Governor's Mansion, I sometimes think about what it was like at the first dinner served in the dining room in 1907. World War I had not happened yet, however in 1917, ten years after the Governor's Mansion was built, France was flooded with American soldiers.

By the early twenties, women's suffrage ushered in many changes in society. Women had the right to vote, the Charleston was "the dance," and dress hems were cut to the knee.

In the 1930s, Alabama experienced an abundant shift to a more conservative lifestyle. The Great Depression, Roosevelt's New Deal and World War II were a part of the lives of all Alabamians. The world's tallest skyscraper, the Empire State Building, was built in New York City and opened to the public on May 1, 1931.

All eyes looked to the newest inventions for entertaining as the Golden Age of Hollywood entered into theaters in small towns and large cities. The full-color films of the 1930s opened the doors of our hearts with **Gone with the Wind, The Wizard of Oz** and more than twenty other classics released in 1939. What a wonderful time to live!

The 40s were pressed between the radical 30s and the conservative 50s. World War II news came across the airwaves by radio each night as families gathered around the dinner table. I can imagine the scene on that Sunday, December 7, 1941, when the words rang out from the radio, "Pearl Harbor has been attacked by the Japanese!" I can see the families in this neighborhood getting ready for Sunday church services as people ran out on the lawn to comfort neighbors and try to comprehend the fact that World War II was declared. On December 2, 1945, we were free from this war, which is still known as the most destructive armed conflict in human history.

April 12, 1945, more news could be heard as windows were raised to allow cool spring breezes to circulate throughout the Montgomery home here on South Perry Street. Many home-owners were working in their yards and enjoying a beautiful spring day. Suddenly, the news was heard throughout the world, that President Franklin Roosevelt was dead. As he sat for his portrait painting, he collapsed, suffering from a massive cerebral hemorrhage and died later that day.

I was born a month after World War II ended. Much of the 40s are memories told to me by my parents. However, the 50s came alive to me as a little girl who can remember getting our first television set. "Howdy Doody Time," "The Honeymooners" and "I Love Lucy" were my favorites. We enjoyed our television set, but every Saturday night we still tuned in to "Amos and Andy" on the radio. It would be safe to say our Governor's Mansion, in 1950, would have heard the beautiful music of "Mona Lisa" by Nat King Cole, "Harbor Lights" by Sammy Kaye and the "Tennessee Waltz" by Patti Page on the radio and on records. Yes, I've been asked many times, "Don't you wish these walls could talk?" Well, only if I could hear the 1950 top charts of "Music! Music! Music!"

by Teresa Brewer, and "If I Knew You Were Comin' I'd've Baked a Cake" by Eileen Barton. Those are the voices I'd love to hear.

Things were made easier for women in the home with the invention of the automatic washing machine and Mixmasters. Paper towels became the new luxury in the kitchen in 1931. The microwave oven came on the scene in very upscale and modern kitchens in 1954.

Most women stayed home and were homemakers and mothers. The Donna Reed days would soon be gone for many as the 60s, 70s, 80s and 90s became a part of our lives.

We have seen many governors and first ladies come in and out of this grand home. Each has left their legacy. Each has spent happy days and each has faced difficult days while occupying this home. Each governor and first lady have left behind a part of Alabama's history.

The recipes you will enjoy have come from all fifty states and United States provinces. First ladies and first gentlemen have been so kind to share family favorites or foods they have served at their own Governor's Mansions when the dinner bell rings.

Thank you to all the first families for helping me by sharing a recipe. Thank you for your purchase of this cookbook. The proceeds will go to maintain the Alabama Governor's Mansion and Hill House, the sister house of the Mansion, built in 1910.

I know you will enjoy all of these recipes and keep the dinner bell ringing at "your mansion."

Patsy Riley
First Lady of Alabama, 2008

# When the Dinner Bell Rings at the Governor's Mansion

# Notes

# When the Dinner Bell Rings at the Governor's Mansion

Governor Riley and I have been among the blessed Alabamians who have served this state and lived in this wonderful 100-year-old house we call home and the people call the Governor's Mansion. Guests and family alike always hear the dinner bell ring inviting all who join us for wonderful food and pleasant memories.

Alabama truly is the great hospitality state and it certainly should start at the Alabama Governor's Mansion. This cookbook will give you a glimpse of our dinner table when the dinner bell rings at the Alabama Governor's Mansion.

## "Welcome to Our Home" Punch

*We serve this to all our guests when they first arrive. It's just a nice way to say, "Welcome to our home, the Governor's Mansion."*

1 (2 qt.) bottle white grape juice, cold
½ bottle ginger ale, cold
1 bottle long stem cherries

Mix well, pour in glass and float a long stem cherry.

## Aunt Sara's Hot Seafood Casserole

*This is a favorite of both family and guests. It's one of my stand-bys for Bible study groups for a light luncheon. I serve it in large seashells, usually with one vegetable and a green salad. Sara is a great cook, dear sister-in-law and now has taken Mama's place in looking after me. Thanks, Sara, for all you do and for all your love.*

1 lb. crabmeat, fresh, frozen or canned
1 lb. steamed small shrimp
1 c. mayonnaise
2 T. diced pimento
¼ c. chopped bell pepper
3 c. chopped cooked chicken
½ c. chopped onion
1 c. chopped celery
¾ tsp. salt
2 tsp. parsley
1 T. Worcestershire
2 T. lemon juice
2 c. cracker crumbs
2 T. butter
½ tsp. paprika

Heat one tablespoon butter in skillet. Stir-fry vegetables until thoroughly heated. Remove from heat. Toss all ingredients. Save ½ cup cracker crumbs and mix with butter for topping. Sprinkle with paprika and top casserole with crackers. Bake at 350° for 25 minutes.

Yield: 6-8 servings

# Leslie's Beer Cheese Soup

*Oh, how I love this soup! And oh, how I love my daughter-in-law, Leslie. She is a wonderful wife, mother and homemaker. She knows and understands my heart and that is a wonderful blessing. Thank you, Leslie, for sharing this recipe.*

> 3 c. milk or half & half
> 1 (12 oz.) can beer
> 16 oz. Velveeta cheese
> 1 ½ tsp. Chicken bouillon
> 3 dashes hot sauce
> ¼ c. plus 2 T. flour (plain) or Shake & Blend
> ¼ c. water

Heat milk and cheese slowly until cheese melts. Do not boil. Add bouillon, hot sauce and paste slowly. Add beer slowly. Serve with French bread.

*Tip: For an extra rich soup, use 2 c. half & half and 1 c. milk. Use half & half to make paste. Using Shake & Blend will help keep the lumps out!*

# Beans in a Bundle

*These are so beautiful and delicious on a plate. We serve these quite often because they give a real catering touch to any meal.*

> 1 can vertical packed whole green beans
> Bacon strips
> 1 (2 oz.) jar pimento strips
> 1 (8 oz.) bottle French dressing

Wrap 8-12 bean bundles in ½ strip of bacon. Place in a Pyrex dish, pour French dressing over beans and marinate overnight. Bake in same pan for 25 minutes at 350˚ or until bacon is done. Garnish with pimento strips. Serves 4.

# Aunt Maudine's Marinated Ham

*My Aunt Maudine was a gifted, talented lady. I get my love of fresh flowers from her. She and my Uncle Jimmy Williams owned and operated the Auburn Flower Shop for many years. She loved to entertain. She shared this recipe with me after she prepared this wonderful meat at her lake house in 1970. Fresh watermelon fruit salad, fresh corn on the cob and Beans in a Bundle make this an excellent meal.*

> 3 to 4 ham steaks or thick breakfast ham
> 1 c. brown sugar
> 1 ½ c. red cooking wine or cooking sherry
> 1 jar peach pickles
> 1 jar red apple rings

Cut ham into serving size pieces. In an oblong casserole dish, add brown sugar, sherry, juice from pickles and apple rings. Stir to dissolve brown sugar. Place ham in juice. Marinate for at least one hour or longer turning every 20 minutes. Meat should be turned often during the soaking process. Cook over a low heat charcoal grill, turning three or four times. Cook about 15 minutes.

*Tip: Any leftovers are great with eggs and hot biscuits the next morning!*

# Homemade Peach Ice Cream

*I remember the hot June morning I told the staff I was going to make homemade Chilton County peach ice cream. Their eyes lit up like children at Christmas. Some of the staff who didn't know me that well looked at me with confused looks on their faces, "You are the First Lady. You aren't supposed to be cooking for us!" Well, they soon learned my greatest joy is cooking for others and bringing joy into someone's life in "cool" ways… like homemade ice cream!*

 4 to 6 eggs
 3 c. sugar
 2 T. vanilla
 4 c. half & half
 ½ pt. whipping cream (not whipped)
 6 c. whole milk
 4 c. peaches, chopped in blender or puree
 ½ c. peaches, chopped coarsely (optional)

Beat eggs and sugar together in a large bowl until well blended. Add vanilla and beat. Slowly add half & half and whipping cream and milk. Add the peaches. Pour into electric freezer tub. Freeze according to directions. This can become strawberry ice cream by substituting fruit or it's great plain.

*Tip: Adjust sugar to your family's taste, more or less! If you don't care for a real creamy ice cream, leave out whipping cream.*

# Date, Pecan and Bacon Roll-ups

*I love to serve these and watch the looks on our guests' faces. No one can decide what it is. Everyone loves them, but no one knows it's a date.*

 1 lb. bacon
 Pecans
 8 oz. pkg. pitted dates

Cut pecan halves in half. Stuff pecan in dates. Wrap with ½ a slice of bacon. Stick with toothpick and broil on a cookie sheet until brown.

*Tip: Cut as many pecan halves as you need to stuff dates.*

# Pork Tenderloin Marinade

*Our very first dinners, our very first days in Montgomery, Lucile Waller came to my rescue. She was working with us and she had a fabulous marinade for pork. This is a very easy, quick and delightful way to serve pork tenderloin. Lucile was just what God ordered in my early days. She and I became fast friends as we worked together to get the mansion ready to reopen just a month after we arrived. It was hard work, but somehow we made it fun. She is my sister in Christ and I am so blessed to have her in my life. Thank you, Lucile, for always being an encourager!*

 2 pork tenderloin
 1 jar apricot preserves
 1 bottle light Teriyaki sauce

Mix preserves and sauce in bowl. Marinate meat for 5 to 6 hours. Grill slowly. We serve warmed raspberry or apricot preserves with this meat.

*Tip: You may need additional Teriyaki and preserves.*

## Aunt Sara's Crock Pot BBQ

*This is an absolutely great recipe! It's so helpful to be able to cook it all day or night in the crock-pot and have it ready for lunch or dinner without much fuss. It's nice to have on hand for drop by friends and family. Together Sara and I have raised 9 children and we have helped raise 18 grandkids. We need quick food with no fuss!*

2 onions
1 (4-5 lb.) boneless Boston butt
16 whole cloves
1 ½ c. water
2 bottles of your favorite BBQ sauce

Slice 2 onions. Salt and pepper Boston butt, place in crock pot and top with sliced onion. Push 6 cloves into top of butt. Sprinkle the rest on top of meat. Pour ½ c. of water into pot. Cook for about 8 hours on low or until pork is tender and falling apart. (I usually put mine on at night and cook until morning.) Take out of pot. Pull pork apart removing all fat. Clean pot of all juices. Put pork back into pot. Pour BBQ sauce over pork and stir. I sometimes add ½ c. of the juice from the cooked pork. Spoon onto hamburger buns. Baked beans and chips fit nicely with these sandwiches.

*Tip: If you do not like much sauce, place plain meat back into pot. Then let folks add bar-b-que sauce to their sandwich, as much or as little as they like.*

## Mama Verna's Frozen Parfait Salad

*We are blessed that one of our four parents lived to see Bob become governor of our great state, my sweet mother, Verna Sumners Adams of Ashland, Alabama. She loved this salad on hot summer days. It's great with any type of meat or alone with crackers. Many times I've served this at the mansion and people think it's a dessert!*

1 c. salad dressing (Bama)
1 can (1 lb. 14 oz.) fruit cocktail, drained
Bananas
Pineapple tidbits
⅓ c. sugar
1 pkg. (8 oz.) cream cheese
1 ½ c. miniature marshmallows
½ c. chopped pecans
1 c. whipping cream, whipped
Few drops of food coloring

Gradually add sugar and softened cream cheese to salad dressing. Whip until fluffy. Mix a few drops of food coloring (green, red, or yellow) until well blended. Fold in well drained fruit cocktail, marshmallows, nuts and whipped cream. Spoon mixture into a large casserole dish and freeze. This may also be frozen in salad molds.

*Of course, my favorite color for this salad is pink. Just add food coloring for your favorite color.*

# Peachy Alaga® Chicken

*Speaking of Chilton County peaches grown in Alabama, add another wonderful product made in Alabama, Alaga® Syrup and Alaga® Hot Sauce. Mix with chicken and a few other ingredients and you'll have a dinner everyone will be raving over. And it's really quick to fix.*
*I give Chef Clayton Sherrod all the credit for creating this great dish. I got to cook it on public TV on a wonderful show with Jackie Galassini and Virginia Whitfield of Whitfield Foods. This was featured in Taste of the South, Fall 2004.*

> 1 ½ lb. skinless, boneless chicken breast, cut into large diced pieces
> 1 (1 ½ oz.) package dry onion-soup mix
> 1 (10 oz.) bottle Russian salad dressing
> 3 T. The Original Alaga® Syrup
> 2 T. Alaga® Hot Sauce
> 4 oz. peach-cobbler jam or peach preserves
> 2 T. cornstarch
> 2 T. butter
> 4 large peaches, peeled and sliced*
> 1 large sweet onion, peeled and sliced
> Cooked rice

Preheat oven to 350˚. Place chicken in a greased 4-quart casserole dish. In a bowl, combine soup mix, salad dressing, Alaga® Syrup, Alaga® Hot Sauce, jam and cornstarch. Stirring until blended. Pour over chicken. Cover dish and bake for 1 hour. Melt butter in a large skillet over medium heat. Add peach slices and onion slices. Sauté until onion is tender. Pour over baked chicken. Serve over rice.

*If fresh peaches are not available, substitute 1 (29 oz.) can of sliced peaches (drained).*

# Hot Cocoa

*Time stands still for no man. Children grow up and soon we are doing things for our grandchildren that we did a few years ago for our own babies. In the wintertime when our kids were growing up, I made hot cocoa every morning before they left for school. I loved taking a hot cup upstairs while they studied in bed or sitting by the fire at night with the girls when things weren't going too well in life. Somehow, that cup of cocoa with a big marshmallow and a nice talk with Mom helped make things better. Now, early mornings on the weekends and holidays when we are together as a family, the little ones and I make sure hot cocoa is ready for our cartoon time. It warms all our tummies and they warm my heart- all 7 of them! Soon it will be 8!*

> ¼ c. cocoa
> ½ c. sugar
> Dash salt
> ½ c. water
> 4 c. milk or half & half
> 6 marshmallows

Combine cocoa, sugar and salt in saucepan. Add water and bring to a boil, stirring constantly. Boil for two minutes. Add milk. Stir and heat. Serve with marshmallows.

# Homemade Lemonade

*We are so happy to be able to open the Governor's Mansion for tours. More than 68,000 guests have come through the front door. It's our delight to serve lemonade on the back patio overlooking the Alabama shaped pool. We can't always make our lemonade from scratch, but here is a recipe for a little less than 68,000!*

> 6 lemons
> 1 to 1 ½ c. sugar
> ½ gal. water
> Red or yellow food coloring

Boil sugar and water until dissolved. Set aside. Squeeze lemons. Add juice to water. Add 1 or 2 drops of red food coloring to get the desired "pink." Serve on a hot summer day with your grandchild!

# Ice Cream Dessert

*We love this dessert! It's easy. It's great year-round, and your family and guests will think you have been working on this for hours!*

> 1 box ice cream sandwiches
> 1 bottle caramel ice cream topping
> 1 large container frozen
> whipped topping, thawed
> 2 c. chopped nuts
> 3-4 crushed Heath bars

Unwrap ice cream sandwiches and place in a 9x13 inch pan. Pour caramel topping evenly over sandwiches. Spread whipped topping over caramel. Top with nuts and Heath bars. Cover and freeze for at least 1 hour before serving. Cut into squares, then drizzle with hot fudge sauce (see Hot Fudge Sauce, page 21).

# Sunday Dinner Ham

*I love to smell a ham cooking in the oven. A ham cooking at the mansion just gives the whole house a "homey" feeling.*
*This is a wonderful Sunday dinner. It will make your mouth water just looking at this masterpiece. My mother-in-law, Elizabeth Riley, gave me this recipe as it was her son Bob's favorite. I served this to our family on Bobby's dedication Sunday, in memory of his great grandmother, Nanny Riley.*

> 1 boneless ham
> 1 small jar orange or apricot
> preserves
> 1 can Coke
> 1 c. brown sugar

Place ham in Dutch oven. Spread preserves on ham. Sprinkle with brown sugar. Pour half Coke slightly on ham. Use the rest to cover bottom of pan. Bake 1 ½ hours on 325°, or a slow, low heat.

> Ham Sauce:
> ½ c. brown sugar
> 3 T. cornstarch - paste
> 1 c. raisins
> Excess ham juice

When ham is cooked, pour off the juice into a saucepan or double boiler. Add ½ c. brown sugar, 3 T. cornstarch and 1 c. Raisins. Cook until the sauce thickens. Serve in sauce bowl along side the ham. Spoon over sliced ham.

*Tip: Juice should be cool before adding cornstarch and raisins. I mix together a small amount of water and cornstarch.*

# Best Ever Vegetable Casserole

*Every time I cook this for any and all dinners, everyone goes back for seconds and even thirds. This is by far my favorite vegetable casserole!*
*You can make it several days ahead. And you can also make it a meal by itself. I just love it!*

1 can white shoe peg corn, drained
1 can French style beans, drained
1 can celery soup
½ c. shredded sharp cheese
½ c. chopped celery
½ c. chopped onion
¼ c. chopped bell pepper
½ c. sour cream

Topping:
½ box cheese crackers, crushed
½ stick melted margarine
½ c. slivered almonds

I have found cooking the vegetables is not best. Just layer in an oiled casserole dish the corn, french beans, celery, onion and bell pepper. Do not mix. Layer these raw vegetables. Then in a bowl, mix sour cream and celery soup. If you like it real creamy, it may take 2 cans soup and 1 c. sour cream. Spread on top of layered vegetables. Top with cheese and then topping. Cook until bubbly, about 20 minutes at 350˚.

*Tip: Sometimes I like to toast my almonds in butter and add to dish after it has cooked. Your almonds need to be golden brown.*

# Laura's Banana Nut Bread

*One of the first things our kitchen staff learned to bake when we arrived in Montgomery was Banana Nut Bread. This is great to keep on hand as it freezes wonderfully. It is nice to have cream cheese ready to spread on top of this bread. Laura Wigfall does a beautiful job of baking this bread and makes sure I have it for all my meetings at the mansion, along with cheese straws.*

½ c. shortening
½ c. butter
3 c. sugar
2 tsp. vanilla
4 eggs
¼ tsp. salt
3 ½ c. flour
2 tsp. soda
½ c. buttermilk
6 small very ripe bananas, mashed
1 c. chopped pecans

Cream shortening, butter, sugar and vanilla until fluffy. Add eggs one at a time, blending thoroughly after each addition. In a separate bowl, sift salt, flour and soda twice. Add dry ingredients to the creamy mixture, alternating with the milk. Combine bananas and nuts and blend into mixture. Pour into greased angel food pan. (Two 9x5 inch greased loaf pans can also be used.) Cook in a 350˚ oven for 1 hour and 10 minutes.

# MaMaCile's Cheese Straws

My dear friend Lucile Waller has shared a very special and classic recipe with me that I would like to share with you. This cheese straw recipe comes from her grandmother whom she called MaMaCile from Butler County, Alabama. Lucile told me that she remembers "pressing out," by hand, hundreds of cheese straws, so many that you could probably fill a Greenville warehouse! I am grateful for friends like Lucile and I love to listen to those special memories she shared with her grandmother.

> 1 stick butter
> 1 lb. New York State Sharp Cheddar Cheese (Grated)
> 2 cups of plain flour
> ½ teaspoon of salt
> Little (2 dashes or so) Worcestershire Sauce

Let stick of butter and cheese come to room temperature and then combine. Gradually work in 2 cups of flour and ½ teaspoon of salt into cheese and butter mixture. Lucile did this by hand, but now you can use a food processor! Add 2 or so dashes of Worcestershire. Put mixture in a cookie press and turn out on an ungreased cookie sheet. Cut the cheese straws with a small knife so they are about 3 1/4 inches long. Growing up, Lucile's cookie press had a narrow lengthwise opening with the top edge being serrated. Bake in a 350° oven for about 20 minutes, until _very slightly brown_. Place on the middle shelf of oven for baking. While still warm, sprinkle lightly with salt. Keep these in tins covered with tin foil to keep crisp.

# Pink Tuna Congealed Salad

This is a great luncheon salad. It's light and cool, so it's very good for hot muggy days in the south. It's pink, so it's great for weddings, bridesmaids parties or luncheons. I've served this several times and everyone asks for the recipe. This comes to me from Julia Butts, a dear friend for 35 years from Ashland days. Julia is one of those friends, if you had a headache and there was only one aspirin in this world and that aspirin was in New York City, she'd go to New York City and get you that aspirin. What a friend! This recipe came from Julia by way of her sweet mother, Dawn Prestridge, from Cullman, Alabama.

> 1 Env. plain gelatin
> 1 can tomato soup
> 1 pkg. (8 oz.) cream cheese
> 1 c. mayonnaise
> ⅓ c. chopped green bell peppers
> ½ c. chopped celery
> ⅓ c. chopped onions
> ½ c. pickle relish
> 1 can tuna, drained
> Sliced green olives are good in this too.

Soften gelatin in ½ c. warm water. Heat soup, add cream cheese and mix well. Add gelatin to this and stir in mayonnaise. Add the remaining ingredients. Chill till firm. This keeps really well for several days.

# Strawberry Crêpes

*It's been said throughout the state that these crêpes sealed the deal with the world renowned German company ThyssenKrupp. I personally cooked this dessert when we had the ThyssenKrupp Company here for lunch as they decided between Alabama and Louisiana. I think it was a lot more than the crêpes, but I was happy to do my part in getting ThyssenKrupp to our great state.*

> 3 eggs
> 1 ½ c. all purpose flour
> 1 tsp. sugar
> ⅛ tsp. salt
> 1 ½ c. whole milk
> 2 T. melted butter or oil, cooled

Using a rotary beater, beat eggs about a minute on medium speed or until yellows and whites are well blended. Add half the dry ingredients and mix well. Then add remaining dry ingredients. (If mixture is too thick for beaters, add a small amount of milk.) Add a little milk at a time until half is used. Beat a moment, then pour in remainder and beat until smooth. Beat in melted butter. Set aside for 1 or 2 hours or refrigerate overnight and cook later. Place in small skillet about 5 or 6 inch on medium heat. Brush with butter or oil and lift off heat. With ladle, pour 1 ½ to 2 T. batter, (only enough to coat bottom of pan). Swirl in the pan quickly. It will start to lift at edges. Peel off and lay out on waxed paper or use an electric crêpe maker (**like I do!**) Or look for ready-made crêpes at your grocery store!

**Strawberry Filling: This is the easy part.**
1 carton strawberries (fresh)
1 c. Sugar
½ pt. whipping cream
1 c. Brown Sugar

Wash and slice strawberries. Place in a bowl. Sprinkle with sugar and set aside. Beat ½ pt. whipping cream, the real thing, not Cool Whip.
Place brown sugar in a small bowl. This will make it easier to sprinkle.

In the center of each open circle crêpe, brown side down, sprinkle 2 T. brown sugar, ¼ c. strawberries or 3 full spoonfuls and 1 scoop whipping cream. Close circle. If you are having problems making them close, use less whipping cream and strawberries. Put a tiny bit of whipping cream and a whole or half strawberry in the center to garnish. Or use canned whipped cream for garnish only. A mint leaf will also add to this gorgeous dessert.

*Tip: Having an extra helper to serve as soon as crêpes are made will ensure your dessert doesn't become a little soggy. These need to be eaten as soon as they are made.*

## Kim's Strawberry Pretzel Salad

*I love to serve interesting food as well as delicious to the taste buds. This will be a nice conversation salad at your next dinner, luncheon or church covered dish event. Kim Nall has been wonderful as our special events coordinator. She has brought talent, energy and commitment to the Governor's Mansion. She shared this salad in our earliest days in Montgomery and we've served it many times. Thanks Kim, for all you did for our special events and tours. You truly made every event special!*

Pretzel layer:
2 c. pretzels, crushed
½ c. sugar
¾ c. butter, melted

Cheese layer:
1 (8 oz.) package cream cheese, softened
1 c. sugar
1 (10 oz.) carton whipped topping

Topping:
1 (6 oz.) package strawberry Jell-O
2 c. boiling water
2 (10 oz.) packages frozen strawberries with juice

Mix pretzel ingredients together and spread in 9x13 inch pan. Bake at 350° for 10 minutes. Cool completely.
Mix middle layer ingredients together and spread on top of cooled pretzel layer. Dissolve Jell-O in boiling water. Add strawberries. Let partially set. When Jell-O mixture is partially firm, spread on top of cheese layer and chill thoroughly.

## Hot Chicken Salad Sandwiches

*Again, this is a very different recipe. I love the crunch of these neat sandwiches. Kids love these, also. One rainy spring day, I had my granddaughters and several of their cousins join me for a production of "The Secret Garden" at the Shakespeare Festival. We were planning a picnic after the theatre. Due to the rain, we had to spread our blankets inside and the girls enjoyed their sandwiches and tea party on the floor. It made for a nice memory for us all. This recipe came to me from my Aunt Kathryn Adams of Ashland, Alabama.*

5 eggs, well beaten with 3 ½ T. milk
1 hen, cooked and chopped
1 small jar pimento
1 small can water chestnuts, sliced
2 T. onions
1 can celery soup
1 can mushroom soup
20-24 slices of sandwich bread
1 medium bag potato chips

Mix all ingredients. Cut crust off bread. Spread mixture on bread to make sandwiches. Freeze. Dip each frozen sandwich in the well-beaten egg mixture. Roll in the crushed chips. Bake at 300° for 50 minutes or until golden brown. Cut and serve.

*Tip: Bake right from the freezer. Do not thaw before rolling in chips.*

# Calypso Pie

*For all chocolate lovers, this dessert has won the blue ribbon with our guests. It's truly death by chocolate and what a way to go! This comes from Becky Gaither Boddie, our childhood friend from Ashland, Alabama. Becky is a friend that is always there. If not there physically, she is there in thought and spirit when the joys and sorrows come along.*

> ½ pkg. Oreo cookies
> ½ gallon vanilla ice cream
> 1 small carton Cool Whip

Slightly crush cookies and line two 9 pie pans with cookie crumbs. Fill with softened ice cream. Top with Cool Whip and freeze.

> Hot Fudge Sauce:
> 2 c. sugar
> 2 T. cocoa
> 3 T. cornstarch
> ⅓ tsp. salt
> 2 c. water
> ½ stick butter

Mix all ingredients in a heavy boiler. Cook at medium heat until it bubbles and becomes thick. Cool for 15 minutes. Drizzle over individual slices of pie.

*Tip: The longer you cook it, the thicker it gets.*

# Chicken Salad Ambrosia

*At one of my speaking events, the ladies of the church served this chicken salad recipe. I never thought I'd ever taste a chicken salad as good as my mother's recipe of 50 years, but this one comes close.*

> 2 c. cooked chopped chicken breast
> 1 c. chopped celery
> 1 11 oz. can mandarin oranges
> 1 c. green or red seedless grapes halved
> ½ c. chopped pecans
> ¼ c. mayo
> ¼ c. sour cream
> 1 ½ tsp. dry Italian salad dressing mix

Makes 4 cups. Mix ahead and chill for seasonings to flavor.

*Tip: One medium can pineapple tidbits gives this recipe a tropical flavor.*

*Prepared by Brenda Campbell from her Granny Sue Wynn's recipe for the GracePointe Church Ladies' Quarterly Dinner - Patsy Riley Guest Speaker May 27, 2004, Montgomery, Alabama. Thank you ladies for sharing your recipe with me. We've served it and enjoyed it at the mansion. It's now our stand-by chicken salad for all occasions.*

## Mama's Fried Chicken

*Southern Fried Chicken- there is nothing better and every southern gal needs to be able to cook it right. So here's a recipe that will make you so glad you are from Alabama, the Heart of Dixie. I served this great fried chicken at a church dedication for our fifth grandchild, Wilson. Family members said it was the best fried chicken they had ever eaten. Of course, that brought smiles to this Mama's face.*

> 8 boneless chicken breasts or strips
> 2 eggs, beaten
> 1 qt. buttermilk
> 6 c. self-rising flour
> Salt (to taste)
> 1 bottle Wesson oil

Beat eggs in large bowl. Add buttermilk and blend. Add chicken that has been washed well to milk mixture. Marinate meat for 30 minutes. Roll one piece at a time in flour. Fry in hot oil until golden brown. Salt to taste.

*Tip: I use a Fry Daddy. I find it works best. Good luck, girls!*

## Annie Maude's Great Grape Salad

*Human love and the delights of friendship out of which are built the memories that endure. How we treasure the many friends we've had to come and enjoy the Governor's Mansion. My family loves this salad recipe. We've also served this refreshing dish as an appetizer before the main course at dinner. This could also be a great summer dessert.*

> 2 ½ lbs. red seedless grapes
> 2 ½ lbs. white seedless grapes
>
> Cream:
> 1 (8 oz.) cream cheese
> ½ c. sugar
> 1 8 oz. sour cream
> 1 c. chopped toasted pecans
> ½ c. brown sugar, on top of last layer

Wash, drain and dry grapes on paper towel. Make cream mixture and set aside. Layer each mixture in casserole or bowl starting with white and ending with red grapes. Make a layer of ½ red grapes. Top with cream mixture and then ½ white grapes. Make layers of grapes and cream mixture, ending with red grapes. Top with remaining cream mixture. Sprinkle with brown sugar. Top with 1 c. chopped toasted pecans. Chill well before serving.

# Lemon Cheesecake Squares

*On November 2, 2008, for the unveiling of* When the Dinner Bell Rings at the Governor's Mansion, *my staff and I decided to serve sweet treats from this cookbook to all who came for our unveiling reception. Lucile Waller, the mansion administrator, found this delicious Lemon Cheesecake Square recipe while flipping through the pages of* Southern Lady *magazine. This particular recipe comes from the March/April 2008 edition and we hope you enjoy it as much as we have.*

1 ¼ c. all-purpose flour, divided
½ c. confectioners' sugar
1 c. butter, softened
½ c. finely chopped unsalted cashews
2 pkgs. (8 oz.) cream cheese, softened
2 ¼ c. sugar, divided
½ c. milk
1 tsp. lemon extract
4 large eggs
⅓ c. fresh lemon juice
2 tsp. lemon zest
½ tsp. baking powder
Garnish: confectioners' sugar, raspberries, lemon zest

Preheat oven to 350°. In a medium bowl, combine 2 cups flour and confectioners' sugar. Using a pastry blender, cut in butter until mixture is crumbly. Stir in cashews. Press mixture evenly into bottom of a 13x9 inch baking pan. Bake for 15 minutes.

In a medium bowl, combine cream cheese and ½ cup sugar. Beat at medium speed with an electric mixer until smooth. Add milk and lemon extract, beating until well combined. Pour over crust. Bake for 15 minutes. Remove from oven and cool for 10 minutes. In a medium bowl, whisk together 1 ¾ cups sugar, eggs, lemon juice and lemon zest.

In a small bowl, combine ¼ cup flour and baking powder. Add to sugar mixture, whisking to combine. Pour over cream cheese mixture. Bake for 40 minutes or until a wooden pick inserted in center comes out slightly sticky. Cut into squares and garnish with sugar, raspberries and lemon zest, if desired.

# When the Dinner Bell Rang for Alabama's First Families

*Notes*

# When the Dinner Bell Rang for Alabama's First Families

*Our lives are on a journey, and we may not pass this way again. So hold on to the moment and do all that you can. For though grace is sufficient for the day, moments, like eagles, fly away. –Nancy Veldman*

As the Governor's Mansion's 14h First Lady, I'm thrilled to be able to share a portion of this cookbook with other first families. To hear their dinner bells ring at the Governor's Mansion, we go back in time to days and dinnertime with these past first ladies. We've certainly had some impressive guests to sit at our table.

## Governor and Mrs. Gordon Persons

*Elizabeth Persons Killingsworth, daughter of Governor Gordon Persons, contributed some of her mother's favorite recipes. Elizabeth said, "When Papa (Gordon Persons) was inaugurated in January of 1951, I was a teenager attending Sidney Lanier High School on Court Street. My father was a native of Montgomery and prior to moving to the mansion we resided on Laurel Lane in Cloverdale. We were the first family to live in the present Governor's Mansion. Rather than having an Inaugural Ball, Papa decided to have a reception for all the people so that they could view the new facility. I remember people being lined up for blocks on Perry Street. It was a beautiful affair. During their term of office, Mom and Papa would gladly provide the residence for school functions. My friends were always welcome. A few years ago, I attended my 50th class reunion and among the collected memorabilia were many pictures of my classmates taken at the mansion. One of my father's favorite hobbies was building and flying gasoline driven model airplanes. In fact, it was only years later that I realized that most of what I thought were 'boyfriends' were really there to fly planes. Because Mom and Papa were great listeners, all my friends really enjoyed their company."*

## Persons' Chicken Salad

    8 large halves chicken breasts
    Celery leaves
    Parsley and few onion slices
    1 or 2 lemons
    1 c. celery hearts, chopped fine
    1 c. mayonnaise
    1 T. Durkee Famous Sauce
    Salt (to taste)

Wash chicken breasts and place in heavy pot with celery leaves, onion slices and parsley. Add water to cover and add salt. Simmer until well done and tender. Cool in broth before removing meat from bones. Cut into small pieces. Mix celery, mayonnaise, Durkees and chicken. Toss gently. Add salt. Adjust amount of mayonnaise as you like it. Chill.

Yield: 8 servings (generously)

*Suggested Menu: Chicken Salad, Fresh Fruit with Poppy seed Dressing and Cheese Straws or Pimento Cheese sandwiches.*

# Persons' Pimento Cheese

3 pkgs. (8 oz.) New York sharp
Cheddar cheese - at room
temperature
½ onion, grated
2 (4 oz.) jars diced pimentos,
drained
½ to ⅔ c. of Hellman's
mayonnaise

Grate cheese. Grate onion on top
of cheese. Add pimento. In electric
mixer, combine grated cheese, onion
and pimento with ⅔ cup Hellmann's
mayonnaise. Start by adding ½ cup of
mayonnaise and gradually adding the
additional mayonnaise until desired
consistency. Mix until smooth but
thick enough to spread evenly. Serve on
rounds of sandwich bread or crackers.
Keeps in refrigerator for several weeks.
*Note: The grated onion is the secret
ingredient.*

# Governor Persons' Favorite Tomato Wiggle

*This was the Persons' favorite
summertime open face sandwich.*

1 slice bread or English muffin
1 T. mayonnaise
1 to 2 sliced peeled tomatoes
Salt and pepper to taste
½ tsp. finely grated onion
2 strips bacon, cooked and
drained
New York sharp Cheddar
cheese, grated, to cover

Preheat oven to 350˚. Toast bread
or muffin lightly so that it isn't soggy.
Spread with mayonnaise and top with
tomato slices. Sprinkle with salt and
pepper. Scrape grated onion over top.
Top with bacon and grated cheese on
top. Bake 5 minutes or until cheese
is melted. Some prefer to broil slowly
until cheese is melted.

Yield: 1 serving

# First Lady Persons' Lane Cakes

*The original recipe came from The Blue Moon Cookbook. However, First Lady Persons made a few changes, one of which was adding more bourbon. She often made these for St. John's Episcopal Church Bazaar where they were very popular.*

Bake cupcakes from yellow cake mix or your own scratch recipe. Hollow out center of each cupcake with a paring knife. Fill hollowed center with about 1 tablespoon Lane Filling. Ice sides of cake with your favorite white icing.

Lane Filling:
4 egg yolks
½ c. granulated sugar
½ stick butter, melted
¼ c. maraschino cherries, chopped
¼ c. bourbon
1 ½ c. pecans, chopped fine
½ c. raisins, chopped
¼ c. pitted dates, chopped

Beat yolks and sugar together and add butter. Cook in top of double boiler over low heat, for about 10 minutes or until thickened. Add bourbon. Cool and stir in fruits and nuts. Use as filling for cakes.

# Persons' Best Icebox Cookies

*First Lady Persons kept the dough in the refrigerator and would slice and bake for after school snacks for her children.*

1 c. butter, softened
1 c. sugar
1 c. light brown sugar
2 eggs
1 tsp. vanilla
1 c. chopped nuts (pecan)
½ tsp. baking powder
½ tsp. baking soda
½ tsp. salt
3 ½ c. all-purpose flour

Cream butter and sugars. Beat in eggs and vanilla. Sift together flour, salt, baking soda and baking powder. Add to creamed mixture. Fold in nuts. Shape into 2 long rolls, 1 ½ inches in diameter. Wrap in waxed paper. (Dough freezes well.)
Refrigerate overnight. Thinly slice dough and place on ungreased cookie sheet. Bake at 350° for 10 minutes.

Yield: 5 dozen

## Persons' Brown Sugar Dessert

*This recipe came from the Persons'
Aunt Georgia Persons who lived in New
Orleans. A great winter dessert!*

2 eggs
¾ c. flour
2 - 3 tsp. vanilla
1 ½ c. chopped pecans
1 ½ pt. whipped cream (need
some for topping)
1 tsp. baking soda
2 c. brown sugar

Beat eggs. Add sugar. Sift flour and
soda and add to egg mixture. Fold
in vanilla and pecans. Divide into 2
greased and floured 8 inch cake pans.
Bake 350° for 25 minutes. Cake will
rise and fall. If it starts to brown too
much on edges, reduce heat to 325°.
When cool, crumble and combine
with whipped cream. The consistency
is like soft ice cream. Serve in silver
compotes or serving dishes. Top with
whipped cream and a cherry.

## First Lady Persons' Favorite Ice Cream with Chocolate Sauce

*First Lady Persons served a variety of
desserts, although this was her favorite.
Usually served in a silver compote with
vanilla ice cream and topped with the
following sauce. Serve with a mocha
cake or cookie.*

Chocolate Sauce:
½ c. butter
2 ¼ c. confectioner's sugar
⅔ c. evaporated milk
½ tsp. Almond extract
5 squares bitter chocolate

Combine butter and sugar in top of
double boiler. Heat until butter is
melted and mixture is creamy. Add
chocolate and milk. Continue to cook
over hot water for 30 minutes, but do
not stir while cooking. Remove from
heat. Add almond extract and beat with
spoon. Serve over ice cream while still
warm. Store leftovers in refrigerator
and reheat as needed.

Yield: 1 ½ pints

# Persons' Mocha Cakes

*Make your own angel food cake or buy it from a bakery. Cut cake into small squares 2 x 2 inches or larger if you like. With a metal spatula, generously ice cakes on 4 sides and top with Mocha Icing. Roll in coarsely ground peanuts. Refrigerate cakes in hot weather.*

Mocha Icing:
1 lb. box 10x confectioners' sugar
2 sticks butter
1 T. Instant coffee
1 16 oz. can peanuts

Dissolve coffee in 1 tablespoon cool water. Cream butter until light and fluffy. Add sugar in small amounts beating well after each addition. When half the sugar has been added, mix in small amounts of the coffee alternately with the remaining sugar. Continue beating until fluffy. Ice cakes. Roll in peanuts.

*Note: Add 1 tablespoon of cocoa for extra flavor. Can add more coffee if desired.*

# Governor and Mrs. Jim Folsom, Sr.

## Cream Cheese Pound Cake

1 pkg. (8 oz.) cream cheese, softened
½ c. margarine
½ c. butter
3 c. sugar
6 large eggs
3 c. cake flour
1 tsp. vanilla extract
1 tsp. almond flavoring

In a large mixing bowl, cream butter, margarine, sugar and cream cheese. Add eggs, one at a time, beating well after each addition. Add flour, vanilla extract and almond flavoring. Mix well. Pour into a greased and floured 10 inch tube pan. Bake at 325° for about 1 hour and 30 minutes or until cake tests done. Cool in pan 10 minutes before removing.

# Governor and Mrs. John Patterson

*There were many momentous occasions centered around a wonderful meal at the dining room table while the Pattersons were in office. Finding these recipes has elicited numerous memories for Governor Patterson. Guests such as Dr. Wernher von Braun, described a journey to the moon to former legislators and the annual Alabama Cattleman's Association banquet with Gunsmoke stars James Arness (the Sheriff), Amanda Blake (Kitty), and Dennis Weaver (Chester)!*

## Governor Patterson's Favorite Pork Roast with Braised Vegetables

> 3 lbs. boneless pork roast
> Salt and pepper
> Carraway seeds
> 1 sliced onion
> ½ bunch parsley
> 3 sliced carrots
> 12 small onions
> 12 small potatoes or 6 medium ones
> 3 stalks of celery

Preheat oven to 425˚. Season the roast with salt and pepper and carraway seeds. Set the pork roast in a shallow roasting pan and bake at high heat until the fat begins to brown-about 20 minutes. Add a cup of water (as much as needed to create a sauce) and then heat to 325˚. Bake until tender, about another hour or so.

While the pork is roasting, peel the onions, potatoes and carrots. Wash the celery stalks. Set a large pot of salted water to boil. Cut the carrots and celery into two or three pieces. If the potatoes are medium sized, cut them in half. When the water comes to a boil, drop in the vegetables and cook until they are almost tender and drain them. Set aside until the roast has cooked for an hour and is almost ready. Add the parboiled vegetables to the pan and let them finish cooking with the roast.

Serve on a large platter with the roast surrounded by the vegetables and any extra sauce on the side. This is delicious with a crusty loaf of French bread and a green salad tossed with a light lemon and olive oil dressing.

# Governor George Wallace and Governor Lurleen B. Wallace

*Contributed by Peggy Wallace Kennedy as published in* The Governor's Favorites, *"...a trusty guide to learn about your Governors and a must for the cookbook collector's shelf (1965)."*

## Governor Lurleen's Favorite Carrot Cake

2 c. plain flour
2 c. sugar
2 tsp. salt
2 tsp. soda
2 tsp. cinnamon
1 ½ c. Wesson oil
4 eggs
3 c. carrots, grated

Sift flour, sugar, salt, soda and cinnamon together. Add Wesson oil. Add eggs, one at a time beating well after each addition. Add the carrots. Grease and flour two cake pans. Bake 40 to 50 minutes in a 325° oven.

Frosting:
2 small packages cream cheese
1 box confectioners' sugar
1 stick oleo minus 1 tsp.
2 tsp. vanilla
1 c. ground pecans

Soften cream cheese and oleo. Blend well and add the confectioners' sugar a little at a time. Add vanilla and nuts.

## Governor George Wallace's Favorite Brunswick Stew

1 lb. pork
3 boneless chicken breasts
1 lb. beef
3 medium size onions
Salt, pepper, Accent, catsup and Worcestershire sauce to taste
1 tsp. sugar
1 can corn
2 cans tomatoes
3 medium size Irish potatoes
1 T. vinegar

Cook meats together until tender. Cut in very small pieces. Add other ingredients and cook slowly for one and one half hours.

# Governor and Mrs. Albert Brewer

*The tradition of fine southern cuisine and elegant entertaining was certainly not lost on our family. We grew up with our mother who enjoyed cooking and was so good at it. She taught us the art and importance of presentation and taste. Equally important were exemplary lessons of manners and social grace. During our school years, we were welcomed home daily with warm cookies, cake or pie. Alison and I continued that tradition when our own children were young. It is not unusual for Alison, myself, the grandchildren, Mary Martha, Katie, and Preston to prepare Mother's tried and true recipes and to entertain friends and family with the grace and poise she taught us. The tradition continues.*

*- Becky Brewer Cooper*
*These wonderful recipes were given by the Brewer's daughters, Rebecca Brewer Cooper and Alison Brewer Calhoun.*

## Governor Brewer's Ground Beef Patties

> 2 lbs. ground beef
> 2 T. chopped parsley
> ⅔ c. celery, chopped fine
> ¼ c. grated onion
> 1 tsp. salt
> ½ tsp. pepper
> 1 ½ T. Worcestershire
> 2 tsp. Accent
> ½ tsp. celery salt

Mix together lightly until well blended. Overmixing or mashing makes patties tough. Shape into small, flat patties. Brown in very small amount of hot oil in heavy iron skillet. Pour off fat after cooking all patties. Deglaze pan with small amount of butter and water or sherry for au jus to ladle over meat.

## Brewer's Curried Fruit

> 1 (29 oz.) can pears
> 1 (29 oz.) can peaches
> 1 (29 oz.) can apricots
> 1 can pie cherries
> 1 (16 oz.) can chunk pineapple
> ½ c. butter
> ¾ c. brown sugar, packed
> 4 tsp. curry powder

Drain fruit and arrange in baking dish. Melt butter. Add sugar and curry to butter, blending well. Pour mixture over fruit. Cover and refrigerate for 24 hours. Uncover and bake for 1 hour.

Yield: 8–10 servings

# First Lady Martha Brewer's Ambrosia

2 dz. large navel oranges
1 (28 oz.) can crushed pineapple, optional
¾ c. Angel Flake coconut
½ cup maraschino cherries
1 oz. cherry juice
¾ c. sugar, vary according to sweetness of oranges

Peel oranges. Section, being very careful to remove all membrane. Cut sections into small pieces. Add other ingredients and cover. Refrigerate overnight before serving.

# Brewer Family Connoisseurs' Casserole

1 (12 oz.) can shoepeg corn, drained
1 (16 oz.) can French-style green beans, drained
½ c. chopped celery
½ c. chopped onion
1 (2 oz.) jar pimentos, drained
½ c. sour cream
½ c. sharp Cheddar cheese, grated
1 can cream of celery soup
½ tsp. salt
½ tsp. pepper

Mix together all the above ingredients together. Pour mixture into a 9x13 inch casserole dish.

Topping:
1 c. Ritz crackers
½ c. slivered almonds
¾ stick butter, melted

Combine these ingredients and pour over casserole mixture. Bake on 350° for 45 minutes.

Yield: 8 servings

# Brewer Family Christmas Salad

*This salad was not only served with Christmas dinners at the Governor's Mansion, but at many meals throughout the year.*

1 (6 oz.) lime Jell-O
1 c. boiling water
2 T. lemon juice
1 (15.5 oz.) can crushed pineapple, with liquid
½ c. sugar
1 c. grated cheese
½ pt. whipping cream
½ c. pecans, chopped

Boil lemon juice, pineapple, and sugar for 3 minutes. Remove from heat. Dissolve Jell-O into 1 cup boiling water. Add the lemon mixture. Pour mixture into a 9x13 inch dish. Put into refrigerator. When mixture begins to thicken, add grated cheese, whipped cream and nuts. Cover and refrigerate.

## Governor Brewer's Sunday Dinner Chicken Pot Pie

*This was a staple for Sunday dinner in the Brewer Family home.*

½ c. cold chicken broth
½ c. flour
1 ½ c. hot chicken broth
2 ½ c. stewed chicken, coarsely chopped
¾ c. drained LeSeur peas
¾ c. diced celery
1 tsp. salt

Make a paste by blending cold chicken broth and flour until smooth. Add paste to the hot chicken broth cooking over direct heat. Stir constantly until sauce boils and thickens. Combine with chicken, peas, celery and salt. Pour into a 2 quart casserole dish. Cover with a pie crust. Pierce the crust with a fork. Bake in 425° oven until the crust is nicely browned.

## Brewer's Refrigerator Pickles

8 c. sliced cucumbers
3 c. sugar
2 c. vinegar
1 green pepper, sliced
1 onion, sliced
1 T. celery seed
5 tsp. non-iodized salt

Boil vinegar, sugar and salt. Pour over cucumbers, pepper and onion. Refrigerate in jars for 6 weeks before using.

## Brewer's Best Stuffed Peppers

4 large green peppers
½ stick butter
⅔ c. onion, chopped fine
1 lb. lean ground beef
1 c. canned diced tomatoes, drained
2 T. Worcestershire
2 c. cooked rice
Salt and pepper to taste
¼ c. bread crumbs, buttered

Cut out stem end of pepper and cut in half. Remove the seeds and white membrane. In a heavy skillet, heat the butter and sauté beef and onions until beef is browned. Add tomatoes and continue cooking until liquid is absorbed. Remove from heat and stir in rice, Worcestershire, salt and pepper to taste. Stuff peppers and top with buttered breadcrumbs. Place in a shallow baking pan with about ¼ inch of water. Bake at 350° for about 20 minutes or until browned. Serve with Creole sauce.

Creole Sauce:
1 medium onion, chopped fine
1 medium green pepper, chopped fine
2 T. butter or margarine
2 c. canned diced tomatoes, drained
1 c. chili sauce
1 tsp. salt

Sauté onions and peppers in butter until tender. Add tomatoes and salt. Simmer 20 minutes. Add chili sauce and simmer another 10 minutes. Pour over peppers.

# Governor Brewer's Roast Beef Casserole

2 c. leftover roast beef (cut in bite-sized pieces)
½ c. chopped onion
½ c. chopped celery
½ c. chopped green pepper
2 T. butter
2 T. soy sauce
2 cans cream of chicken soup undiluted, or 1 can cream of chicken soup undiluted, and 1 can cream of mushroom soup undiluted
1 can water
⅛ tsp. Tabasco

Set oven at 325˚. In skillet, cook onion, green pepper and celery in butter until limp (about 10 minutes). Do not brown. Remove vegetables from skillet. Cook beef until brown. Mix all ingredients. Pour in 2 quart casserole dish. Cover and bake 30 minutes. Remove cover and bake 10 minutes longer. Serve over rice. This casserole freezes well.

Yield: 6 - 8 servings

# Governor Brewer's Favorite Strawberry Angel Pie

*This angel pie is one of Governor Brewer's favorite desserts. It has been enjoyed by many dinner guests and family.*

Pie Shell:
3 egg whites
1 tsp. cream of tartar
1 c. sugar
10 soda crackers, crushed
1 c. chopped pecans

Beat egg whites and cream of tartar until stiff. Slowly add sugar. Fold in the crackers and pecans. Pour into a buttered pie pan. Bake 30 minutes at 350˚.

Filling:
½ pt. heavy cream
½ c. sugar
1 pt. sliced strawberries

Beat cream until it peaks. Beat in sugar. Fold in strawberries. Pour mixture into cooked pie shell. Refrigerate. Serve with a dollop of sweetened whipping cream.

# Brewer First Family German Chocolate Cake Icing

*This is the first thing Rebecca Brewer Cooper learned from Mrs. Brewer. She made a German chocolate cake for the high school bake sale every year.*

3 egg yolks
1 c. sugar
1 can evaporated milk
1 stick butter
1 c. pecans
1 c. coconut
1 tsp. vanilla

Melt butter in large saucepan. Add sugar and evaporated milk. Stir until smooth. Add beaten egg yolks. Continue stirring over low heat. Add pecans and coconut, stirring until mixture is thick. Remove from heat. Add vanilla. Spread on tops of each layer. Use a box German chocolate cake mix for your cake.

# First Lady Brewer's Kum-Bac Dressing

½ c. oil
1 tsp. black pepper
1 tsp. salt
2 c. mayonnaise
¾ c. chili sauce and catsup mixed
1 clove garlic, grated
1 tsp. Worcestershire sauce
1 tsp. prepared mustard
Juice from 1 lemon
2 T. water
1 dash Tabasco
1 dash paprika

Mix all ingredients well and store in refrigerator.

# First Family Squash Casserole

1 to 1 ½ lb. squash
1 medium onion, finely chopped
2 slices of bread soaked in milk
1 egg, slightly beaten
2 to 3 T. butter
1 tsp. salt
Dash pepper
1 ½ c. grated cheese

Wash squash. Cut ends off. Slice squash into 1 to 1 ½ inch slices. Cover with water and cook until tender. Drain. Mash with butter, salt and pepper. Add egg, bread and onion. Mix well. Pour half of mixture in casserole dish and top with half of cheese. Add remaining mixture and top with remaining cheese. Bake at 350˚ for 30 minutes.

# Governor and Mrs. Fob James

## Fob, III's Fried Flounder

*Given by son of Governor and Mrs. Fob James, Fob James, III.*

Flounder filets
Milk
1 c. pancake or waffle mix
1 c. white cornmeal (stone-ground is best)
Vegetable oil

Either cut the flounder filets in half down the spine, or cut them into chunks, depending on if you are frying them in a skillet or in a Dutch oven. Place filets in a shallow baking dish. Pour enough milk to cover. Let sit 15 minutes. In a Ziploc bag, combine pancake mix and cornmeal. Heat one inch of oil in a skillet or several inches for a Dutch oven, until medium hot. If you are unsure of the correct temperature, you can toast a bread cube in the oil. At the correct temperature, a bread cube will take 60 seconds to toast. Shake the fish a few pieces at a time in the Ziploc bag until thoroughly coated. Cook about 5 minutes per side in the hot oil. Be careful not to crowd the skillet or the pan. Remove fish when it is golden brown, drain on paper towels, and keep hot in the oven until all is cooked.

*Suggestion: Serve with slaw, new potatoes, and hush puppies.*

Yield: 6 servings

# First Family James' Gee Gee's Yeast Cake Biscuits

*Given by daughter-in-law of Governor and Mrs. Fob James, Beth James. This was the original recipe of Governor James' mother, Rebecca James, affectionately known as Gee Gee.*

 1 c. vegetable shortening
 2 l. sugar
 1 packet yeast
 1 tsp. salt
 1 tsp. baking powder
 1 tsp. baking soda
 1 tsp. cream of tarter
 1 ½ c. buttermilk

Dissolve the yeast in a scant ¼ cup of warm water. Cream shortening and sugar well. Sift the flour and measure four cups, slightly scant. Sift again with salt, baking soda, baking powder and cream of tarter. Add to shortening with buttermilk. Mix well and add yeast. Cover and let rise in warm place until doubled in bulk. Mash down and refrigerate dough or roll out. Dough can be refrigerated up to two days, but must be brought back to room temperature before rolling out (that takes several hours). Roll out and cut with biscuit cutter. Place in a lightly greased pan. Let rise and bake at 425° until lightly brown. To prebake, do not let biscuits brown. Cool completely and double wrap to freeze.

*Note: I recommend tripling this recipe when you make it and stocking the freezer. Thaw frozen biscuits in the fridge.*

Yield: 12 servings

# Governor James' Pavlova

*Given by daughter-in-law of Governor and Mrs. Fob James, Beth James.*

 4 egg whites, room temperature
 ¼ tsp. salt
 ¼ tsp. cream of tarter
 1 c. sugar
 4 tsp. cornstarch
 2 tsp. white wine vinegar
 1 tsp. vanilla extract
 1 c. cream, chilled
 3 c. strawberries, sliced
 3 tsp. Grand Marnier

Sprinkle strawberries with sugar and Grand Marnier. Set aside. Preheat oven to 275°. Beat egg whites, salt and cream of tarter together until egg whites hold a stiff peak. Add the sugar, a few tablespoons at a time, beating all the while until the mixture is stiff and glossy. Beat in cornstarch, then vinegar, then vanilla.
Butter and flour an 8 inch cake pan. Gently fill with meringue, spreading it higher around the edges than the center.
Bake one hour to 1 ¼ hours until meringue is firm and lightly brown. Cool. Lightly whip cream.
To serve, slice meringue in pie shaped slices, top with berries, and finally whipped cream.

Yield: 6 servings

# First Lady James' Apple Scones

*Given by daughter-in-law of Governor and Mrs. Fob James, Beth James.*

¼ c. apple juice
½ c. currant (may substitute raisins)
½ c. apple dried and chopped
1 c. buttermilk
¼ c. sugar
3 T. butter, melted
2 c. flour
1 T. baking powder
1 tsp. baking soda
¼ tsp. salt
¼ c. walnuts, chopped (optional)

Preheat oven to 350°. Place apple juice in a bowl and microwave 3 minutes. Add dried apples and currants. Let sit at least 15 minutes. This can sit overnight in the refrigerator.

Combine buttermilk, sugar, butter and apple juice mixture in a large bowl. Lightly spoon flour in a dry measuring cup. Level with a knife. Combine flour, nuts (if desired), baking powder, soda and salt. Add buttermilk mixture and stir until just smooth.

Drop into 12 rounds on a baking sheet coated with cooking spray. Bake 17 minutes until golden.

Yield: 6 servings

# Governor James' Boursin Cheese Spread

*Given by daughter-in-law of Governor and Mrs. Fob James, Beth James.*

1 clove garlic, minced
2 (8 oz.) packages cream cheese, softened
1 c. butter, softened
1 tsp. oregano
¼ tsp. basil
¼ tsp. dill weed
¼ tsp. marjoram
¼ tsp. thyme
¼ tsp. black pepper

Place herbs and garlic in the food processor. Process until chopped. Add cream cheese and butter. Pulse until evenly blended. Do not over process. Refrigerate.

*Yield: 10 servings*

*NOTE: Measurements are for dried herbs. Whenever possible, use fresh herbs and change quantities to two tablespoons oregano and one teaspoon of each of the other herbs, chopped. Herbs such as tarragon, parsley, and chervil can also be added or substituted.*

# James Family Best Chiles Rellenos Casserole

*Given by daughter-in-law of Governor and Mrs. Fob James, Beth James.*

1 lb. ground round steak or ground turkey
1 c. onion, chopped
1 tsp. cumin
1 ½ tsp. oregano
2 cloves garlic, chopped
¼ tsp. salt
¼ tsp. black pepper
1 (16 oz.) can refried beans fat-free
1 (4 oz.) can green chilies, chopped and drained
1 c. Monterey jack-colby cheese, pre-shredded
1 c. frozen corn, thawed and drained
⅓ c. flour
¼ tsp. salt
1 ⅓ c. milk
Dash hot pepper sauce
2 eggs
2 egg whites
Cilantro, chopped

Preheat oven to 350˚. Cook ground beef (or turkey), onion and garlic until meat is brown. Drain well. Add next five ingredients (cumin through beans). Set aside.

Sprinkle half the chiles in a baking dish. Top with ½ cup cheese, then the meat mixture. Top with corn, then remaining chiles, then remaining cheese.

Combine flour and salt. Gradually add remaining ingredients, except cilantro, stirring with a whisk until blended. Pour over the casserole. (Casserole may be made to this point and refrigerated overnight.)

Bake for 1 hour and 5 minutes or until set. Let stand 5 minutes before serving. Serve with cilantro sprinkled on top.

Yield: 6 servings

# First Lady Bobbie James' Doreen's Special Rice

*First Lady Bobbie James' holiday recipe, served often for her family.*
*This can be served with many things, such as duck, quail, leg of lamb, etc.*

4 c. wild rice (cooked)
1 onion
1 red pepper
1 yellow pepper
1 green pepper
2 stalks celery
1 c. fresh mushrooms
½ c. pine nuts
1 can water chestnuts, sliced
2 T. olive oil
6 slices bacon

Chop onion, red, yellow and/or green peppers, celery, fresh mushrooms, pine nuts and/or water chestnuts. Sauté in olive oil 5 to 10 minutes in saucepan on top of stove until done. Fry bacon crisp and break into small pieces. Add the mixture. Salt and pepper to taste. Mix with cooked wild rice for a Sunday night meal! Northern Waters Wild Rice needs to be soaked overnight before cooking for best results.

## Governor James' Best Apricot Roasted Chicken and Vegetables

2 carrots, peeled and cut on the diagonal in 1 inch pieces
2 beets, peeled and cut into wedges
1 squash, acorn variety, cut in wedges
1 parsnip, peeled and cut on the diagonal in 10 inch pieces
1 fennel, cut in wedges
2 T. olive oil
1 tsp. olive oil
¼ c. apricot jam mixed with 2T water
2 T. thyme
4 chicken breasts
½ lemon, cut into wedges

Heat oven to 450˚. Toss vegetables with 2 tablespoons oil and 2 table-spoons jam mixture. Add thyme and season with salt and pepper. Spray 13 x 9 inch pyrex dish. Roast for 10 minutes.

Heat remaining oil in a skillet over medium-high heat. Salt and pepper chicken. Brown on both sides, about 5 minutes per side. Place chicken on top of the vegetables. Roast 15 more minutes. Pour the remaining apricot jam over the chicken and continue roasting until chicken and vegetables are tender (about 15 more minutes). Arrange meat and vegetables on plates and pour the juice over them.

*Note: This is a delicious winter recipe. It can be prepared quickly if the vegetables are prepared earlier during the day. Serve with wild rice. Serve with baked apples with Spiced Ricotta for dessert.*

# Governor and Mrs. Jim Folsom, Jr.

## Folsom's Roasted Mediterranean Vegetable and Chicken Salad

*This recipe was served at an event honoring Heather Whitestone, Miss Alabama, just prior to her leaving for the Miss America Pageant. To our delight, she captured the crown and won the title.*

4 oz. balsamic vinegar
1 tsp. garlic, minced
3 tsp. Dijon mustard
⅔ cup olive oil
½ tsp. salt
1 tsp. sugar
½ tsp. black pepper
1 lb. chicken breast, roasted and cubed
1 lb. red potato, small, cut in half
1 lb. eggplant, cut into 1 inch cubes
1 head garlic, peeled and roasted, optional
¼ c. olive oil
1 red onion, cut into 6 equal wedges
2 red bell peppers cut into 1 inch squares
8 oz. fresh green beans
6 oz. marinated artichoke hearts, drained
½ c. black olives, pitted
1 c. fresh basil, chopped
½ c. fresh parsley, chopped
8 oz. cubed feta cheese

Prepare the vinaigrette by mixing the first seven ingredients together. Mix well and set aside.

Toss the potatoes in ¼ cup of the olive oil and place in a roasting pan. Toss the cubed eggplant in the remaining oil and place in a separate roasting pan. Place both pans in a 375˚ (preheated) oven. Roast the eggplant for about 15 minutes. Remove from the oven and cool. Continue cooking the potatoes an additional 15 minutes or until tender. Remove from the oven and cool.

Combine all the ingredients together in a large bowl, pour the vinaigrette over the mixture and toss well to distribute the vinaigrette. Refrigerate until serving time.

# Governor Jim Folsom's Favorite Chicken Marbella

*This recipe is a Folsom family favorite.*

> 10 lbs. meaty chicken pieces
> 1 head garlic, peeled and finely pureed
> ¼ c. oregano
> ¼ tsp. salt
> ⅛ tsp. black pepper
> ½ c. red wine vinegar
> ½ c. olive oil
> 1 c. pitted prunes
> ½ c. pitted Spanish green olives
> ½ c. capers with a bit of juice
> 6 bay leaves
> 1 c. brown sugar
> 1 c. white wine
> ¼ c. fresh parsley, chopped

In a large bowl, combine first 11 ingredients. Cover and let marinate overnight in the refrigerator. Preheat oven to 350˚.

Arrange chicken in a single layer in one or two shallow baking pans and spoon marinade over it evenly. Sprinkle chicken pieces with brown sugar and pour white wine around them.

Bake for 50 minutes to one hour, basting frequently with pan juices. Chicken is done when pieces pricked with a fork at their thickest areas yield clear yellow (rather than pink) juice.

With a slotted spoon transfer chicken, prunes, olives and capers to a serving platter. Moisten with a few spoonfuls of pan juices and sprinkle generously with chopped parsley. Pass remaining juices in a sauceboat.

*Note: To serve cold, cool to room temperature in cooking juices before transferring to a serving platter. If chicken has been covered and refrigerated, allow to return to room temperature before serving. Spoon some of the reserved juice over chicken.*

# First Lady Marsha Folsom's Chinese Roasted Pork Tenderloin with Red Currant Sauce

*This recipe was first served at an event for Winston Groom, the author of Forrest Gump. It was served at a reception held soon after the release of the movie based on his book.*

Marinade:
1 T. sherry
2 T. soy sauce
3 T. sugar
1 ½ tsp. salt
2 pork tenderloins

Red Currant Sauce:
4 T. sugar
2 T. soy sauce
6 T. white rice vinegar
2 T. yellow prepared mustard
1 T. sesame oil
3 T. red currant jelly
1 tsp. cornstarch
2 tsp. roasted sesame seeds
Green onions, chopped (For garnishing)

Prepare the tenderloins. Mix the sherry, soy sauce, sugar and salt. Pour the mixture over the tenderloins and marinate for a minimum of 2 hours.
To roast, put tenderloins on rack above 1 inch of water. Cook in 350° oven for approximately 40 to 45 minutes. Refrigerate overnight (optional).
Prepare sauce. Mix together the sugar and soy sauce with the white rice vinegar.
Separately, mix the yellow prepared mustard (do not substitute any other variety), sesame oil, red current jelly and cornstarch.
Combine the two mixtures together in a sauce pan. Place over low heat until the mixture thickens slightly. Remove from heat and add the toasted sesame seeds. Serve the sauce on the side or may pour over tenderloins, slice and serve.

*Note: Slice tenderloins on the diagonal, garnish with chopped green onions.*
*Can be served with foccacia or pita for appetizer sandwiches.*

# Parties, Parties and More Parties...

# Notes

# Parties, Parties and More Parties...

*One of the greatest parts of entertaining at the Alabama Governor's Mansion is getting to meet so many wonderful caterers and their staffs. These next recipes are from dinners and parties we've hosted during our time in office. The special friendships with these chefs are memories I will treasure. Once again, Alabama has it all: mountains, oceans, beaches, music, art, southern hospitality and fabulous chefs!*

## Leslie Bailey and Janet Wheat Silver Spoon Caterers

### Silver Spoon Signature Raspberry Cheddar Mold

> 4 c. shredded sharp Cheddar cheese
> 1 c. pecan pieces
> 1 c. mayonnaise
> 2 stalks of scallions, chopped
> ½ tsp garlic salt
> 1 c. raspberry jam

Combine cheese, pecans, mayonnaise, scallions and garlic salt. If mixture needs to be creamier, add a little more mayonnaise. Shape into a heart shape, pressing the center to form a well. Spoon raspberry jam into the center. Serve with crackers.

## Donna Balzaratti The Basket Case Café

*Governor Jeb Bush (FL), Governor Sonny Perdue (GA) and Governor Bob Riley (AL) had a meeting in Dothan, Alabama. Donna and her team at The Basket Case Café served the governors lunch. After leaving, Governor Perdue's security called Hal Taylor, Governor Riley's Security, to ask about the cornbread salad. The Governor said it was the "best stuff" he had ever had. He was so thrilled with his wonderful lunch that he wrote Donna and her team to share with them his enthusiasm. Our Alabama chefs and caterers are making their mark across the southeast with their southern flair!*

## Cornbread Salad

> 4 c. cold, crumbled cornbread
> 12 oz. can Mexican corn
> 17 oz. English peas, drained
> 1 medium onion, chopped
> 1 medium bell pepper, chopped
> 4 boiled eggs, chopped
> Mayonnaise

Mix the first 6 ingredients together in a large bowl. Add enough mayonnaise to moisten. Serve immediately or refrigerate until needed.

# Beef Wellington a la Mansion

4 (8 oz.) filet mignons
Salt
Pepper
Granulated garlic

Sauce Bearnaise:
1 c. white wine
1 c. tarragon vinegar
4 T. chopped shallots
6 T. chopped tarragon plus 1 T. reserved
3 T. chopped chervil plus 1 tsp., reserved
Pinch of crushed peppercorns
Pinch salt

Other:
6 egg yolks
1 lb., 2 oz. unsalted butter
8 very large button mushrooms
4 5 inch squares of puff pastry
1 T. butter
Pinch black pepper
Pinch of garlic powder
¼ c. red wine

Pat dry and generously season the filets with salt, pepper and granulated garlic on both sides.
Let rest at room temperature before cooking for 1 hour.
Place white wine, tarragon vinegar, shallots, tarragon and chervil in a small pan and reduce by ⅔. Allow to cool. Add 6 egg yolks to cooled mixture. Place sauce in double boiler over very low heat. Whisk 1 pound and 2 ounces of unsalted butter into mixture. (Should cook until thickened but not like mayonnaise.) Strain sauce and add the reserved 1 tablespoon chopped tarragon, the reserved 1 teaspoon chopped chervil and one pinch salt. Keep sauce warm. If it separates, whisk in a few drops of cool water. (Enough sauce for 12 generous servings.)

Spray a baking sheet with nonstick spray. Place the 4 squares of puff pastry on the baking sheet. Score pastry with 4 inch round biscuit cutter being careful not to cut all the way thru the pastry. Bake at 350˚ until puffed very high and golden brown. If using convection oven, use the fan.

Thickly slice 1 large button mushroom per serving or any choice of fresh mushroom. Sauté mushrooms with 1 tablespoon of butter, 1 pinch of black pepper and 1 pinch of garlic powder.

In a large skillet, brown steaks evenly on both sides. Add pinch of salt and deglaze pan with ¼ cup red wine. Keep warm. Cook in batches if necessary. Cook filet on both sides to desired doneness. Place cooked puff pastry square on plate and remove top center portion. Place filet down in the pastry. Top with cooked mushrooms. Ladle sauce over top.

# Scott Berg
# HEAL Recipes

*Chef Berg shared these recipes with me and children from across our state at our HEAL (Healthy Eating Active Living) Alabama Exercise Day held at the capitol in November 2007. After exercising with the Governor and me, Chef Berg taught the children how to make these healthy treats at home. Chef Berg, as well as Christy Swaid of Birmingham and many others, are helping to create healthy children, which in turn creates a healthy Alabama.*

## Watermelon Slush

1 Watermelon
3 c. Ice, crushed

Cut watermelon in half and scoop out the pink part and remove the seeds. Put watermelon in blender with crushed ice and purée for 20 seconds. Stop the blender and pour watermelon slush into a glass and enjoy.

## Mango Lassi

8 oz. plain yogurt
1 ripe mango
2 tsp. sugar
¼ c. water
Ice Cubes

Wash and peel the mango and then cut into cubes. Add the yogurt, mango, sugar and water to the blender. Cover the blender and blend until the ingredients are mixed together. Pour into a glass with some ice and enjoy.

## Yogurt Parfait

2 c. canned pineapple chunks
1 c. frozen raspberries
3 c. vanilla yogurt
1 banana, sliced
⅓ c. chopped dates
¼ c. toasted almonds

Place sundae glass on table and add the pineapple, raspberries, dates, bananas and yogurt in layers. Now sprinkle almonds over the top. You can substitute your own ingredients and make your own kind, also.

## Sela Joseph Bischoff
## Imperial Catering, Inc.

## Ginger Crackles

4 ½ c. all-purpose flour
4 tsp. powdered ginger
2 tsp. baking soda
1 ½ tsp. cinnamon
1 tsp. cloves
½ tsp. salt
1 tsp. white pepper
8 oz. soft butter
4 oz. Crisco
2 ⅔ c. sugar
2 eggs
1 tsp. vanilla
½ c. molasses

Sift all dry ingredients together. In the bowl of a mixer, cream the butter, Crisco and sugar together until light and fluffy. Scrape bowl down and add eggs on low speed. Slowly add vanilla and molasses. Scrape bowl down again and on low speed begin adding sifted dry ingredients together, a little at a time, until mixed.

Wrap in plastic and chill overnight. Shape into logs and freeze for up to a month. Slice each into ¼ inch slices, roll in sugar and place on a greased baking sheet. Bake in a preheated 325˚ oven until crackly and brown. Save old cookies to grind for crumbs for cakes, rolling truffles and etc.

## Chef Clayton Sherrod
## Chef Clayton's
## Food Systems, Inc.

## Alabama Wild Shrimp and Spinach Gratin

2 lbs. fresh Alabama Wild Shrimp
½ c. fresh shallots, minced
2 (10 oz.) packages chopped, frozen spinach
4 cloves fresh garlic
4 T. unsalted butter
2 (8 oz.) cans quartered artichoke hearts, drained
2 c. heavy cream
4 oz. garlic herb cream cheese
1 tsp. kosher salt
½ tsp. white pepper
¼ c. freshly grated Parmesan cheese

In a large frying pan, sauté Alabama wild shrimp, shallots and garlic in butter over medium heat. Add well-drained spinach and artichokes. Briefly cook on low heat. Add cream, garlic herb cream cheese, salt and pepper.
Simmer until cheese is melted and mixture is blended. Remove from heat and fold in the grated Parmesan cheese. Place in casserole dish. Serve warm.

Yield: 12 servings

# Black-eyed Pea Fritters

1 c. flour
½ c. cornmeal
¼ c. grated Parmesan
1 medium yellow onion, peeled and minced
3 eggs, lightly beaten
1 ¼ c. evaporated milk
2 tsp. salt
½ tsp. Cayenne
1 lb. cooked black-eyed peas, chopped
4 oz. smoked turkey meat, diced
1 c. vegetable oil

Mix together flour, cornmeal, Parmesan, onions, eggs, evaporated milk, salt and cayenne in a large bowl. Add black-eyed peas and diced turkey, set aside.
Heat oil in a large non-stick skillet over medium heat. Make 4-5 fritters at a time by spooning 2 tablespoons of the batter for each fritter into the skillet. Using a spatula, flatten each mound into a 3 ½ inch pancake. Fry until bottoms turn golden, about 2 minutes. Flip and continue frying until center is cooked through, about 2 minutes more. As fritters are finished, transfer to paper towels to drain. Repeat process with remaining batter.

Yield: 25-30 fritters

# Grilled Brick Chicken with Moore's Marinade

3 Fryers split (from the back bone)
¼ c. Moore's Original Marinade
¼ c. Kahlua
¼ c. Ketchup
3 T. Original Alaga® Syrup
3 T. Moore's Buffalo Wing Sauce
¼ c. Pineapple Juice
½ c. Chicken broth
⅓ c. White Wine
1 tsp. Worcestershire Sauce
1 tsp. Minced Fresh Ginger
3 Bricks (Wrapped in Foil)

Combine Moore's Marinade, Kaluha, ketchup, Alaga® syrup, Moore's buffalo wing sauce, pineapple juice concentrate, chicken broth, white wine, Worcester-shire sauce and fresh ginger in a large bowl. You may marinate your chicken in the sauce. Grill the chicken turning and basting with the sauce. Remove chicken from the sauce. Place skin side down on grill until crusty brown on both sides. Place the foil wrapped bricks on top of the chicken after placing them on the grill. Move chicken over to indirect heat or in an oven to finish cooking until done. Pour remaining marinade in a sauce pan and reduce over moderate heat. Serve with chicken.

# Grit Pie

¾ c. water
⅛ tsp. salt
¼ c. quick-cooking grits
½ c. (1 stick) butter
1 ¼ c. sugar
2 T. all-purpose flour
3 large eggs, slightly beaten
¼ c. buttermilk
1 tsp. vanilla extract
1 (9 inch) frozen pie shell, thawed
Sweetened whipped cream and strawberries, optional

Preheat oven to 325˚. In a small saucepan, bring the water and salt to a boil. Add the grits and cook for 4 minutes, stirring constantly. Add the butter and cook for 1 additional minute. Set aside and cool slightly.

In a small bowl, stir together the sugar, flour, eggs, buttermilk and vanilla. Slowly stir into the cooled grits. Pour into the pie shell and bake for 35 to 40 minutes or until set. Serve warm or cold with whipped cream and strawberries as a garnish, if desired.

## Evelyn Criswell
## Evelyn's Gourmet Recipes

## Shrimp Asparagus Crescent Pie

*In 1978, at the Pillsbury National Bake Off, Mrs. Evelyn Criswell prepared this "Main Dish." I can't wait to try it, Mrs. Evelyn.*

1 8 oz. can Pillsbury Refrigerated Quick Crescent Dinner Rolls
1 10 ½ or 15 oz. can (1-2 c.) asparagus cuts, well drained or 10 ¼ oz. frozen asparagus cuts cooked and drained
4 ½ oz. can (¾ c.) tiny or broken shrimp, drained
3 eggs, beaten
1 ½ tsp. salt
⅛ tsp. black pepper
½ c. light cream or evaporated milk
1 tsp. lemon juice
10 ¾ oz. can condensed cream of shrimp soup
1 ¼ c. (2 oz.) shredded Swiss or Cheddar cheese

Separate crescent dough into four rectangles. Place in greased 10 inch pie pan or 9 inch square pan. Press over bottom of pan and up sides to form a crust. Flute edges of crust and arrange asparagus and shrimp evenly over crust.

In medium bowl, blend eggs, salt, pepper, cream, margarine, lemon juice and soup until smooth. Pour over asparagus and shrimp.

Bake at 375˚ for 45 to 55 minutes or until crust is deep golden brown and knife near center comes out clean. If crust becomes too brown, loosely cover with foil last 10 minutes of baking. Sprinkle with cheese and let stand 15 minutes before serving.

To make ahead, cover and refrigerate up to two hours and then bake as directed.

To reheat, cover loosely with foil and heat at 375˚ for 15 to 20 minutes.

# Evelyn's Coffee and Spice Cake

*In 1971, this dish became the Award Winning Pillsbury Bake-Off Recipe for Mrs. Evelyn. This fantastic cake was served at the Hannah Home Membership Drive Coffee held at the Governor's Mansion in 2007.*

2 ½ c. all-purpose flour
1 ¼ c. sugar
2 tsp. baking powder
1 tsp. baking soda
1 ½ tsp. cinnamon
½ tsp. ground cloves
3 eggs
⅓ c. hot coffee
¾ c. Pillsbury Coconut/Pecan (or Coconut/Almond) Frosting
1 c. (½ pt.) sour cream
¾ c. butter, softened

Glaze:
1 ½ c. powdered sugar
2 T. hot coffee
1 T. butter, softened

Preheat oven to 350˚. Grease and flour a 10 inch bundt or tube pan. In large bowl, combine all ingredients. Beat 3 minutes at medium speed, scraping bowl occasionally. Pour into prepared pan. Bake at 350˚ for 60 to 65 minutes or until toothpick comes out clean. Cool cake upright in pan for 15 minutes. Remove from pan and cool completely. If desired, drizzle with glaze.

# Evelyn's Sun Dried Tomato Torte

2 (16 oz.) rolls goat cheese
4 sticks (1 lb.) butter
6 pkgs. (8 oz.) cream cheese, softened
1 c. basil pesto
1 pkg. (3 ½ oz.) sun dried tomatoes

Place cheeses and butter in a large mixing bowl. Mix until light and fluffy. Add ⅓ cup pesto and blend well. Grease a 10 inch cake pan and line with plastic wrap, extending wrap out on all sides of pan. Layer one third of cheese mixture into bottom of cake pan. Cover with half of remaining pesto, top with another layer of cheese and remaining pesto. Top with remaining cheese mixture and smooth to edges of pan to seal. Cover with sun dried tomatoes cut into small pieces and press down into cheese. Cover with plastic and chill in refrigerator over night until firm. When ready to serve, turn out by pulling on plastic wrap to free from pan. Cut into 8 equal wedges. Serve with Crostini bread that has been brushed with garlic and olive oil.

*I serve this on a three tiered glass stand garnished with sugared green grapes and red pears or strawberries. Enjoyed by all at Christmas time!*

Yield: 25-35 servings

# Evelyn's Tangy N' Spicy Meatballs

4 lbs. ground chuck
2 eggs, beaten
4 c. bread crumbs
2 ½ tsp. onion powder
4 tsp. garlic salt
4 T. Evelyn's Tangy N' Spicy Gourmet Sauce or Evelyn's Original Gourmet Sauce

Mix well and roll into 1 ½ inch balls. Preheat oven to 350˚. Place on greased baking pan and bake for 10 minutes. Remove from oven and turn each meatball. Return to oven and continue baking for an additional 10 minutes or until done. Drain well. Place in crock pot or a 12 x 8 inch baking dish. Cover with 2 bottles of Evelyn's Tangy N' Spicy Gourmet Sauce or Evelyn's Original Gourmet Sauce. Heat until bubbly or heated through. Place into desired serving container.

# Joan Spiess and Rachel Jones Southern Sweets, Inc.

## Wrapped Chicken Breast

*The Wrapped Chicken Breast recipe is Joan's Aunt Eloise's recipe. This is the dish they have served the most throughout their business. It is an instant favorite with most everyone!*

6 - 5 oz. boneless skinless chicken breast
6 slices dried beef
6 slices bacon
1 c. sour cream
1 small can of cream of mushroom soup

Place 1 slice of dried beef on the top of the chicken breast. Wrap the bacon around the entire breast. Lay in baking dish. Do not stack. Bake uncovered for 1 hour on 325˚. Mix cream of mushroom soup and sour cream together. Spread over chicken. (Optional: Drain off ½ of the chicken broth that has formed in the baking dish.) Cover with foil and bake for 1 additional hour. Usually served with rice.

## Southern Sweet Treat Oatmeal Crispy Cookies

*The Oatmeal Crispy Cookie recipe is Joan's mother's that she received while in high school. Her mother will be 80 this year and helps her out LOTS. These cookies go in all of their bagged lunches.*

½ c. white sugar
½ c. brown sugar
½ c. shortening (Crisco)
1 egg
½ tsp. vanilla
½ tsp. salt
½ tsp. soda
¾ c. plain flour
1 ½ c. quick oatmeal
¼ c. pecans or walnuts

Combine sugars and Crisco. Blend very well. Add egg, vanilla and mix. Add dry ingredients. Add oatmeal and nuts. Form cookies on wax paper in a long rectangle loaf. Freeze until ready to bake. Slice off ¼ thickness and bake at 350˚ for approximately 12 minutes.

# Lemon Squares

1 box yellow cake mix
1 egg
⅓ c. oil
1 (8 oz.) cream cheese
⅓ c. sugar
1 T. lemon juice

Mix cake mix, egg and oil together with a fork until crumbled. Take 1 cup out and put aside. Pat remainder into 9 X 13 inch pan. Bake at 350° for 10 minutes. Blend cream cheese, sugar and lemon juice until fluffy. Spread on hot mixture. Crumble reserved cake mix on top. Bake again for 10 minutes. Refrigerate 1 to 2 hours.

# Joel and Kate Wheaton

## Bang Bang Chicken Skewers

*Bang Bang Chicken was served at the Governor's Mansion's Valentine's Party in 2005.*

1 lb. of small prime chicken breast fillets
2 green onions
2 medium red chilies
4 rounded T. of peanut butter
2 T. sweet chili sauce
1 T. soy sauce
½ level tsp. ground cumin
Large pinch of turmeric
24 wooden skewers

Prepare garnish, shred green onions and chilies. Put in iced water for an hour until curly. Next combine peanut butter, chili sauce, soy sauce, cumin and turmeric in a medium bowl with 4 tablespoons of boiling water and stir well. Cut chicken into strips and place in ½ of the marinade for 45 plus minutes. Put the skewers in water to soak. Preheat the grill or broiler. Thread chicken and place on foil lined grill or baking tray. Grill for 5 minutes. Turn and spoon over the rest of the marinade. Grill for another 3-4 minutes until cooked and a rich brown color. Transfer to a serving dish. Drain the garnish and add to the plate.

Yield: about 24 servings

# Shortbread Stars

*The Shortbread Stars have "Starred" in the Christmas parties each year for the Governor and Mrs. Patsy! They add a twinkle to any celebration.*

8 oz. butter
8 oz. flour
5 oz. corn starch
5 oz. fine granulated sugar
Silver dragees (edible silver balls)

Cream butter and sugar. Beat in flour to form firm dough. Wrap and refrigerate for 30 minutes. Roll out and cut star shapes. Push a silver star in the center and bake at 180° for 8 to 10 minutes. Sprinkle with granulated sugar as they come out of the oven. Transfer to wire rack. Cool and enjoy!
Sometimes I add a teaspoon of cinnamon to the recipe and the zest of an orange for a holiday twist.

# Chicken with Sherry Vinegar and Tarragon Sauce

*This dish was served at a dinner at the Alabama Governor's Mansion in March 2005.*

8 pieces of chicken
5 fl. oz. sherry vinegar
15 fl. oz. medium dry, Amontillado sherry
12 shallots, peeled and left whole
4 gloves of garlic left whole
2 T. Olive oil
2 T. tarragon leaves
1 heaped spoon Crème fraîche (Or light sour Cream)
Salt and pepper

Season chicken and brown in batches. Each piece should be a lovely golden brown color. Then remove from the pan. Add the shallots and garlic and brown slightly.

Turn down the heat. Return the chicken to the pan. Scatter the tarragon leaves all over and then add the vinegar and sherry. Let it all simmer for a while. Then turn the heat down low to a slight bubble for about 45 minutes. Halfway through the cooking time turn the chicken to allow the other side to sit in the sauce. When they are ready, remove them to a warm serving dish along with the shallots and garlic. By now the sauce will be reduced and concentrated. Whisk in the crème fraîche and taste for seasoning. Then pour the sauce over the chicken and scatter with sprigs of tarragon. This is lovely served with baby new potatoes tossed in herbs and some fresh shelled peas.

# Butterfly Cakes

*The Butterfly cakes are from the First Lady's Hats and Gloves Tea Party in May 2007.*

4 oz. butter softened
4 oz. fine granulated sugar
2 eggs
1 T. baking powder

For the Icing:
6 oz. butter softened
12 oz. confectioners' sugar, sifted
Confectioners' sugar to dust

Add edible Flower or Small Royal Icing Bees for an additional flourish!

Preheat the oven to 400°. Place paper cases in muffin tin. Measure all ingredients into large bowl and beat well until mixture is well blended and smooth. Half fill cases. Bake for 15 to 20 minutes. Lift from tin and cool on a wire rack. To make the icing, beat butter and confectioners' sugar until light and fluffy. Carefully cut out a circular slice from the top of the cakes. Cut each disc in half. Pipe a swirl of buttercream into the hole and place the half slices of cake back into the buttercream at an angle to resemble butterfly wings. Add garnish if using and then dust with confectioners' sugar.

Yield: About 18 cakes

# Seared Spiced Salmon with a Black Bean Salsa

*The salmon was cooked at a dinner party for Governor and Mrs. Riley in 2006.*

About 2 lbs. salmon
3 fat cloves of garlic
1 ½ inch piece of root ginger
Grated zest of 2 limes (reserve the juice for the salsa)
Pinch of cinnamon
Pinch of ground cumin
½ oz. fresh cilantro, reserve a little to garnish
2 T. olive oil
Freshly milled black pepper

For the salsa:
4 oz. black beans
12 oz. ripe firm tomatoes, skinned and chopped
Coriander
1 medium red onion, finely chopped
1 red chili, de-seeded and finely chopped
1 T. extra virgin olive oil
Juice from the prepared limes in the salmon recipe
½ level tsp. salt

Dry the salmon and remove any visible bones. Place the salmon on a plate. If leaving in one piece, score the surface of the fish slightly to allow the flavors to permeate the salmon. In a pestle and mortar, crush the garlic cloves and salt together. Add the grated ginger, lime zest, cinnamon, cumin, 1 tablespoon of olive oil, chopped coriander and a good grind of black pepper. Mix everything together and massage it into the salmon! Cover with plastic wrap and leave in the refrigerator for several hours or even overnight. To make the salsa, drain and rinse the beans. Add all the salsa ingredients, stir and leave to marinate for several hours. When you are ready to cook the salmon, cut it into your individual portions. Preheat your grill (broiler) to its highest setting. Grease a baking tray and put it in the oven to heat up. Once really hot, don't forget the oven gloves, remove tray from the oven and place the salmon on it. You should hear a sizzle! Position the tray 3 inches from the heat and grill them for exactly 7 minutes. Remove to a warm plate and garnish with salsa and the fresh cilantro.

Jennifer Thompson
Thompson Catering

## Maple Pear Salad

*Yield: 4 servings*

½ container spring mix lettuce, washed and patted dry
2 sweet and ripe pears, thinly sliced
¼ c. chopped walnuts or pecans
½ c. dried sweetened cranberries
¼ c. crumbled blue cheese

In a large bowl, combine lettuce, pears, walnuts or pecans, cranberries and blue cheese. Drizzle with half of Maple Dressing (recipe follows), tossing to coat. Serve remaining dressing on the side.

Maple Dressing:
¼ c. maple syrup
¼ c. olive oil
3 T. balsamic vinegar
1 T. Dijon-style mustard
¼ tsp. ground black pepper
⅛ tsp. salt

In a small bowl, whisk together all ingredients.

## Stuffed Chicken Breast

*Yield: 6 Servings*

3 boneless, skinless chicken breast that have been washed and butterflied to ¼ in. thick slabs
1 pkg. (10 oz.) frozen spinach, thawed and drained very well
1 jar roasted red pepper cut into strips
6 pieces of bacon, cooked to soft stage
6 tsp. Parmesan cheese
1 fresh lemon zested
1 pkg. bamboo skewers or long toothpicks
4 T. olive oil

Preheat oven to 400°. Wash and cut chicken breast, trying not to cut any thin spots. Pat chicken dry with paper towel. Lay chicken cut side up. Salt and pepper chicken. Add 1 piece of bacon to each chicken breast. Add a layer of spinach. Add a layer of red pepper and sprinkle 1 tsp. of Parmesan cheese. Tightly roll chicken breast and secure with skewer or toothpick. Heat oil and lemon zest in skillet on top of stove. Add chicken and brown on all sides. Place skillet in oven to finish cooking until chicken registers 165° on thermometer. Remove chicken from pan and deglaze pan with the juice from lemon. Pour drippings over chicken and enjoy!

# The Riley Family
# Favorites

*Notes*

# The Riley Family Favorites

When I started writing this cookbook, I realized, much to my disbelief, nine years had passed since I started my first cookbook. Many things have changed in our lives, and yet some things are exactly the same. We have added two sons-in-law, three grandsons, two granddaughters and lost one daughter. When I say we've lost Jenice, I quickly add, we haven't really lost her, for we know where she is. She's just not with us in her earthly body, but she is very much with us in spirit.

What has not changed are family favorites; those remain the same year after year. It makes me very happy to cook and bring joy to my family.

Every recipe in this book has a story and a special memory. It is my hope you will enjoy this book and use it to bring your family closer and create some very special memories!

## Easter Sunday Strawberry Bavarian Sponge Torte

*On Easter Sunday afternoon, when the children were small, we'd go to their grandparents to hunt eggs. When Jenice was about 11 years old, my mother made this recipe. She loved it! We all did. I found this recipe on a 1976 calendar at my parents' home this summer. I believe this is where the recipe came from. That is the year Krisalyn, our last baby, was born. Food is so much more than a tummy-filler or nutrients to keep us healthy. Food brings us together and it warms our souls as well as our bodies.*

> 2 pkgs. Strawberry gelatin
> 1 c. boiling water
> 2 pkgs. frozen sliced strawberries, slightly thawed
> ½ pt. whipping cream, whipped (or whipped topping)
> 1 angel food cake, cut in cubes
> Whipped cream to decorate
> Fresh berries to decorate

Dissolve gelatin in boiling water. Add berries and allow to partially thicken. Fold in ¼ pint whipped cream. Toss with cake cubes and place in a greased spring form or angel food pan. Chill torte overnight. Turn out onto a platter and frost with whipped cream. Garnish with whole strawberries. Return to refrigerator until ready to serve.

Yield: 10-12 servings

*Tip: Whipped cream can be tinted pink with a few drops of red food coloring.*

# Rileyhouse Stew – Bob's Favorite

*On cold winter nights, this is still my husband's favorite. Cornbread and fresh corn on the cob will always be a hit at our home.*

2 lb. sm. lean beef cubes or sirloin tips
½ c. Moore's Marinade or Dale's Steak Sauce
½ c. oil
1 pkg. stew seasoning, French's
6 c. water
1 can tomato sauce
1 can stewed tomatoes
10 small potatoes
½ pkg. baby carrots
¼ c. sugar
⅓ stick butter
10 tiny whole onions

Brown beef cubes in hot oil, until each side is browned. Add steak sauce and simmer for 15 minutes. Add stew seasoning and water. Stir. Add rest of the ingredients and cook on low temperature for one hour or longer. More water may need to be added, if you want a soup-like stew. Cook stew on very low heat.

# Rob Riley's Favorite Chocolate Angel Pie

*I always have certain family members in mind when I cook. This pie is all of our favorites, but Rob would eat the whole pie if we'd let him. This has become a favorite when the dinner bell rings at the Governor's Mansion, also. This recipe came to me 40 years ago by way of Goodwater, Alabama. It was passed on to me by Mrs. Vara*

*Thomas, the mother of one of my best friends, Jan Rogers of Alex City, Alabama.*

4 egg whites
dash of cream of tartar
¾ c. sugar
1 tsp. vanilla
18 soda crackers
1 c. pecans, chopped

**Crust:**
Beat 4 egg whites until stiff. Let your egg whites be room temperature before beating. Sprinkle a couple of dashes of cream of tartar while beating. Gradually add ¾ c. sugar. Continue beating to blend sugar. Fold in 1 tsp. vanilla by hand. Crush 18 soda crackers and chop 1 c. of pecans. (I crush and chop before I do any beating because this mixture needs to be ready to go in as soon as egg whites are beaten.) Fold crackers and pecans into egg whites by hand. Do not beat after you add crackers and nuts. Pour into a buttered 9 inch pie pan. Shape and bake in slow oven at 275° until brown. Allow to cool slowly.

*Tip: Egg whites should not be cool, room temperature is best. Also, if you use large to medium eggs, you will get two pie crusts out of one recipe.*

**Filling: 1 pie**
    Mix and chill for one hour:
    ½ pt. whipping cream
    5 T. sugar
    2 T. cocoa
    1 small can coconut for garnish

Beat filling until it looks like chocolate mousse and pour into cooled crust. Garnish with coconut. Store in refrigerator until time to serve.

*When my girls were growing up, I was told, "You can't be their mother and their best friend!" In many ways, now, I find that to be true, but in so many, many ways, I still believe as I did many years ago that the one who loves you and will be the friend who stays closer than any other is your MOTHER! I love you, girls.*

# Minda's Favorite "Birthday Chicken Casserole"

*Minda has had this dish for her special birthday dinner since she was eight years old. I'm so happy she is living close enough that I can cook this great chicken dish for her this birthday! It was given to me by Aunt Maudine of Auburn, Alabama, who taught me my love for flowers. She, also, taught me that no one can load or unload your car for you, for you'll never know where anything has been placed!*

8 boneless chicken breasts
3 c. medium white sauce
1 c. button mushrooms
½ c. white cooking sherry
½ c. slivered toasted almonds

Sauté breast in butter until light brown. Arrange in casserole dish. Add wine to white sauce. Add mushrooms to top of chicken. Pour white sauce over chicken. Bake 1 hour at 325˚. Sprinkle with toasted almonds just before serving. Serve with hot rice.

*Tip: If you are pushed for time, use two cans cream of mushroom soup, omit button mushrooms. Add sherry and pour over chicken. Cook same as the recipe above.*

# Jenice's Favorite Winter Time Homemade Vegetable Soup

*Jenice loved everything I cooked. She was well on her way to becoming a good cook herself. Home and family meant so much to her. She would be so much a part of this life. I know she is so very proud of her Dad and she is loving this cookbook!*

½ lb. beef tips or 3 chicken breasts
1 (16 oz.) can stewed tomatoes
1 (16 oz.) can tomato sauce
1 large onion, diced
3 carrots, sliced
3 ribs celery, sliced
¼-½ head cabbage, sliced
1 can green beans and/or peas and/or
butter peas
1 can corn kernels
3 or 4 potatoes
2 T. sugar
2 T. Moore's Marinade or Dale's
1 (10 oz.) can beef or chicken consomme or cubes
1 stick butter

In a Dutch oven, cook beef tips or chicken breasts on medium to low heat for 1 hour or longer. (One tsp. salt and one tsp. garlic in water while meat is cooking.) Remove meat from liquid. Skim off fats. Add all ingredients and cook for 1 hour or until all vegetables are tender. Pull chicken off the bone or replace beef tips. Place meat into soup. Cook awhile longer on very low heat, until family members arrive home.

# Krisalyn's Favorite "Egg Custard"

*When Krisalyn was growing up, she always wanted egg custard when she was doing her homework. All grown up now, but still loves Mama's Egg Custard. Krisalyn is a wonderful cook and makes this dish for her own little girl, Madilyn Jenice.*

> ¾ c. sugar
> ¼ c. butter
> 4 eggs
> 2 ½ c. scalded milk
> 1 tsp. vanilla
> Pinch of salt

Beat sugar, eggs and butter together until well blended. Add scalded milk, then vanilla and salt. Pour into custard cups and bake until custard is firm and golden brown on top.

*Tip: Top with nutmeg if desired.*

# GiGi's Breakfast

*I will have to add another favorite for the grandchildren. I love to cook a big country breakfast when everyone is home on the weekends or holidays. My grandchildren love their scrambled eggs and bacon. I have a little secret about both. First, I beat my eggs really stiff and then add half & half instead of milk. I beat the eggs again to gets lots of air into them. Salt and pepper to taste. I like to scramble my eggs in butter, not oil. Heat butter until melted, get it hot and pour in those eggs! If you will start your bacon cold, get it to a sizzle and then turn down the heat. Keep turning*

*the bacon. Soon you'll have golden brown bacon. Overcooked and slightly burned bacon or meat of any kind is not healthy eating. Add homemade biscuits and Sorghum, Golden Eagle or Alaga syrup and you've got a truly southern breakfast.*

# Homemade Buttermilk Biscuits

> 2 c. White Lily Self-Rising flour
> ¼ c. shortening
> ⅔ to ¾ c. buttermilk

Preheat oven to 500°. Measure flour into bowl by spooning into measuring cup and leveling off. Cut in shortening until mixture resembles coarse crumbs. Blend in just enough milk with fork until dough leaves side of bowl. Too much milk makes dough too sticky to handle, not enough makes biscuits dry. Knead gently on lightly floured surface 2 to 3 strokes. Roll dough amount ½ inch thick. Cut without twisting cutter. Bake on ungreased cookie sheet (1 inch apart for crusty biscuits, almost touching for soft sides) for 8 to 10 minutes. Serve at once.

Yield: Twelve 2 inch biscuits

*Tip: For tender biscuits, always handle dough gently and use as little extra flour for kneading and rolling as possible.*

*. . . Add cheese grits and you've got a great way to start their day.*

# Cheese Grits

    4 c. boiling water
    1 c. grits
    1 tsp. salt
    1 tsp. onion salt
    1 tsp. garlic salt
    ½ stick butter
    2 c. Cheddar cheese

Bring water to a rapid boil with garlic salt, onion salt and salt. Put in 1 c. grits. Stir well. When grits have thickened, add cheese and butter. Serve with bacon, eggs and homemade biscuits for a great country breakfast or late night supper.

# Riley Grandkids' Fruities-Ba-Tooties

*One of the things I love to do is allow my grandkids to express themselves with the holiday "cookie cookin!" One day, we were baking and we decided to add ingredients I had in my kitchen. We took a basic cookie dough and we added candy sprinkles, M&M's, colored sugars and chocolate sprinkles. We call them Fruities-Ba-Tooties! You could add coconut, cherries, canned pineapples, orange slices, raisins and almonds – just be creative with it. The other ingredient that is a must is lots and lots of giggles! Thanks, Elizabeth for reminding me to put this one in our family favorites!*

# Ren's Breakfast Smoothies

    Frozen fruit (bananas,
    strawberries, raspberries, etc.)
    Plain yogurt (about 1 cup per
    person)
    Honey (to taste)
    Orange juice (to taste)

Blend till smooth. Vary amount of honey depending on whether fruit is sweetened or yogurt is sweetened. We freeze leftover bits of fruit in baggies to make these. You can use fresh fruit, but smoothie will not be thick.

# Rebecca's Raisin Bran Muffins

    6 c. Raisin Bran cereal (15 oz. box)
    2 c. sugar
    5 c. all purpose flour
    5 tsp. baking soda
    2 tsp. salt
    1 tsp. cinnamon
    ½ to 1 tsp. cloves
    ½ to 1 tsp. nutmeg
    4 eggs
    1 c. vegetable oil (can substitute 1 c.
    applesauce for ½ the oil)
    1 qt. buttermilk
    2 tsp. vanilla
    Optional: more raisins and/or
    grated carrots

Mix dry ingredients. Add wet ingredients. Mix by hand. Store in refrigerator until ready to bake. Batter will last up to 4 weeks. Preheat oven to 400˚. Bake for 15 minutes.

# Rebecca, Elizabeth, Ren, Bobby, Wilson and Madi's Favorite "GiGi's Chicken and Dumplings"

*From the time the little ones can climb on a kitchen stool, they learn to cook chicken and dumplings at GiGi's house. What great memories are made in a kitchen! When I asked the grandkids what their very favorite food to eat at GiGi's house might be, it was not much of a debate. All agree that GiGi's Chicken and Dumplings dish is their favorite. I truly am a grateful grandmother.*

*Tip: I continue to learn new ways to make old recipes better. Use half & half to make a smooth paste. Pour very slowly into dumplings. This will give you velvet smooth dumplings.*

> 1 small hen, or 4 chicken breasts with bones
> Water, enough to cover hen
> 1 tsp. garlic salt
> 2 tsp. onion salt
> 1 stick butter
> 1 medium onion, chopped coarsely
> 1 pt. half & half
> 6 c. milk
> Salt to taste
> Pepper to taste
> 2 cans biscuits - Pillsbury Buttermilk
> ¼ c. Pillsbury Shake & Blend flour for paste

Place hen or breasts in a Dutch oven. Fill until hen is almost covered with water. Add salts and ½ stick butter. Cook 45 minutes on medium low temperature; add onions and two celery sticks and cook 15 minutes longer. Remove hen. Bring stock to a full rolling boil. Roll out one biscuit at a time until it is thin and flat. Cut into strips. Add one strip at a time. Cut heat down to low or off. Add half & half and milk. Stir gently. Make a paste with a small amount of flour and water or milk. Add it very slowly to dumpling mixture. If it seems too thick, add more milk. To thin, add more paste. Add remaining butter. You can pull meat off the bone and add to the dumplings or serve the dumplings. Top with meat. Salt and pepper to taste.

*Tip: This is a dish that can be put on hold until everyone comes home for dinner. Be aware when reheating, dumplings burn quickly on bottom.*
*Ren had thirds at Christmas this year. I love to see that at anytime of the year!*

# Ren's Best Monkey Bread

*This has become one of our favorite recipes to cook. Everyone can get in on the fun! Some can cut cubes, others can toss and some can add the sugar mixture. ALL can eat!*

> 4 cans Pillsbury Buttermilk Biscuits
> ½ c. Cinnamon
> 1 ½ c. sugar
> 2 sticks butter
> pecans (optional)

Cut biscuits into cubes, one can at a time. Place in a large bowl. Pour sugar and cinnamon over the dough cubes. Toss and coat well. Drop well coated cubes into well oiled bundt pan. Continue coating cubes. As you finish each can, sprinkle your sugar-cinnamon mixture over the cubes, about ½ c. each time. Alternate cubes and sugar-cinnamon mixture with sliced butter pads. Once you finish all layers, put what's left of butter and sugar mixture on top. Pecans or walnuts can be sprinkled into layers, if you desire. Bake at 325° until it rises and is golden brown on top. It will be slightly hard on top. Let cool for 10 minutes. Then turn out onto cake plate.

*Tip: The more sugar, butter and cinnamon you use, the more syrup that will form as it bakes. When you turn it over and pan is removed, it should glow and be very shiny. Garnish as desired.*

# Elizabeth's Chili

*Elizabeth likes to serve with shredded Cheddar cheese and crackers.*

> 2 pounds ground chuck
> 1 med. chopped onion or 3 T. onion flakes
> 4 (16 oz.) cans beans, und-rained (chili hot and/or kidney beans)
> 1 pkg. Chili O seasoning
> 46 oz. can tomato juice

Brown meat with onions. Drain. Combine with rest of ingredients in large pot (makes about 3 ½ quarts). Bring to boil. Reduce heat and simmer 2 hours, stirring occasionally.

# Krisalyn's Fried Squash

*Krisalyn shares this as one of her favorite dishes from her college days at Montevallo. Even non-squash eaters will ask for seconds!*

> Slice 4 squash, ¼ inch thick
> Dip in 1 egg, beaten
> Roll in 2 c. cornmeal
> Fry in hot oil until golden brown

# Riley Men's Texas Caviar I

*Here's a spicy Texas favorite that's great for Christmas or any holiday. Black-eyed peas and black beans are marinated in a fiery, flavorful mixture. This is great with tortilla chips or bread—and plenty of cold iced tea.*

½ onion, chopped
1 green bell pepper, chopped
1 bunch green onions, chopped
2 jalapeño peppers, chopped
1 T. minced garlic
1 pint cherry tomatoes, quartered
1 (8 oz.) bottle zesty Italian dressing
1 (15 oz.) can black beans, drained
1 (15 oz.) can black-eyed peas, drained
½ tsp. ground coriander
1 bunch chopped fresh cilantro
1 can yellow corn or white shoe peg corn

In a large bowl, mix together onion, green bell pepper, green onions, jalapeño peppers, garlic, cherry tomatoes, zesty Italian dressing, black beans, black-eyed peas, corn and coriander. Cover and chill in the refrigerator approximately 2 hours. Toss with desired amount of fresh cilantro to serve.

# Texas Caviar II

*(Not quite as "hot" as Texas Caviar I and a little quicker to prepare.)*

1 can black-eyed peas (with hot sauce)
1 can shoe-peg corn
½ bottle Italian dressing (4 oz.)
1 small jar salsa or picante (Tostitos Med. 11 ½ oz)
Chopped onion
Pinch of garlic salt
2 or 3 chopped tomatoes

Drain and rinse peas and corn. Mix all and chill at least 2 hours. Serve on tortilla chips.

# Fiesta Hot Bean Dip Casserole

1 (8 oz.) cream cheese
½ pt. sour cream
2 cans refried beans
½ pkg. taco seasoning
¼ c. chopped green onion
½ c. Monterey cheese
½ c. Cheddar cheese

Mix first five ingredients and top with cheese. Bake at 350° until bubbles in the center and cheese browns. Serve with tortilla chips.

# Miss Patsy's
# Alabama Banana Pudding

*During the summer of 1997 at our Annual Congressional Family Picnic, each spouse was asked to bring a dessert with a hint of her state. To my surprise, I won first place for my Alabama Banana Pudding. I was crowned with a chef's hat and my scepter was a wooden spoon. For many reasons I was so thrilled and very surprised to win that night in Washington. When I decided to carry a dessert to the picnic, I didn't have many of the ingredients for most of my great recipes. But I did have 2 bananas, 2 tiny snack boxes of vanilla wafers, a couple of eggs and vanilla. I started working in my kitchen and soon realized - no sugar – oh no! Then I remembered we had just had a fundraiser at our house the morning before. We had plenty of sugar cubes! Well, where there is a will, there is certainly a way. I found a hammer and began to beat those cubes for the pudding. But when it came to my meringue, well, I'd beat with my hammer and then rolled with my rolling pin. Soon those cubes were finely crushed! Jenice and Minda were upstairs wondering what their mother was doing using a hammer to make meringue. Soon they were questioning my sanity over my passion to get that banana pudding cooked for our first Congressional picnic.*

*I'd like to add that my court, second through fourth place winners, were all southern spouses! Great southern women are usually great cooks. I'll say this is my family's "blue ribbon" favorite!*

¾ c. sugar
dash of salt
¼ c. flour
3 egg yolks, beaten
1 T. vanilla
2 c. half & half
2 - 4 bananas, sliced
15 vanilla wafers

Meringue:
3 egg whites
6 T. sugar
2 dashes of cream of tartar
½ tsp. vanilla

Combine sugar, salt, and flour. Add to egg yolk and vanilla in a double-boiler. Slowly add half & half, stirring frequently. Heat until it thickens. Layer wafers and banana slices in 1 ½ qt. baking dish. Add pudding. To make meringue, beat egg whites and cream of tartar for two minutes. Slowly add sugar and vanilla until very stiff. Spread over pudding and bake at 350° until meringue is golden brown!

# Pink Petticoat Asparagus Soup

*Jenice and I loved to go to a tea room in Birmingham. They served a wonderful asparagus soup there. We begged for the recipe, but no luck. One day, I decided I'd play around with this soup recipe. I got it!*

>    2 cans cream of asparagus soup
>    1 ½ to 2 c. half & half
>    1 can chopped asparagus
>    1 pkg. Cheddar cheese,
>    shredded

Place asparagus soup in saucepan and heat slowly. Add half & half, ½ c. at a time and stir. Heat to hot, watch so it doesn't stick. Just before serving, add chopped asparagus. Heat well. Pour into bowls. Top with cheese. You'll love this as much as we did!

# Miss Patsy's Best Ole' Time Candied Yams

>    4 to 6 sweet potatoes
>    1 lemon
>    4 c. sugar

Peel sweet potatoes, wash and cut into halves. Then cut into fourths. Cover with hot water and boil until potatoes are tender. Drain water. Add a small amount of water back to the cooking pot, just enough to cover bottom of pot. Add sliced lemons to water and potatoes. Add 2 c. of sugar. Cook for about 20 minutes. Add 1 more cup of sugar. If potato juice begins to turn to syrup, you may not need the last cup of sugar. If it is very watery, add a small amount of sugar until it turns to syrup.

*Tip: Lemon in the water helps turn your sugar water into syrup. Just let them rest on potatoes when serving. Lemons are not for eating.*

# The Governor's Best Fried Oysters

>    1 to 2 dozen oysters, washed
>    and drained
>    2 eggs, well beaten
>    1 ½ c. half & half or whole milk
>    1 box seafood coating meal

Soak oysters in milk-egg mixture for about 30 minutes. Coat oysters well with meal. Drop one at a time into hot oil. Fry until golden brown.

*Tip: I use Wesson oil and I use my Fry Daddy to keep the heat just right! Cooking about 6-8 oysters at a time. You can use seasoned seafood meal, if you like your oysters a little more spicy.*

# Upside Down Tomato Cornbread

*My family usually likes plain 'ole cornbread, but I do find that variety helps add an element to a meal that is sometimes needed. Here is a really great idea.*

Topping:
2 lg. ripe tomatoes
3 T. vegetable oil
½ tsp. dried oregano
2 tsp. garlic, minced
½ tsp. salt
½ tsp. pepper

Batter:
1 c. yellow cornmeal
1 c. all-purpose flour
2 T. sugar
1 tsp. salt
1 T. baking powder
½ tsp. pepper
1 tsp. garlic, minced
1 small onion, minced
½ tsp. oregano
½ c. Cheddar cheese, grated
1 jalapeño pepper, minced
1 medium egg
⅓ c. vegetable oil
1 c. 2% milk

Core and thinly slice tomatoes, set aside. Preheat oil in a 10 inch iron skillet over medium heat. Sprinkle with oregano and garlic. Place tomato slices in a spiral design overlapping the slices to cover bottom of skillet. Sprinkle with salt and pepper. Reduce heat to low while preparing batter.

Batter: Preheat oven to 400°. In a large bowl, combine cornmeal, flour, sugar, salt, baking powder and pepper. Add garlic, onion, oregano, cheese and jalapeno. Lightly toss mixture. In a small bowl, whisk egg, oil and milk. Stir into dry ingredients. Remove skillet from heat and carefully dot the batter over the tomatoes, smoothing without disturbing the tomatoes. Bake at 400° for 30 minutes or until done. With a large plate on top, flip bread over and let skillet rest for 15 minutes. Cut into wedges and serve while hot.

# First Lady of Alabama: The Things I Love to Cook!

# Notes

# First Lady of Alabama: The Things I Love to Cook!

When I was a little girl, I would come inside on a hot July day and I'd see my Mama cutting off corn for 12:00 lunch. My Daddy would walk home from the drug store, two blocks away on the Courthouse Square. I remember when we sat down for dinner (lunch) I would beg not to have to eat fresh corn! Well… that seems so impossible to me now as I love corn cooked every way it can be cooked!

## Corn Soufflé

*Here is a wonderful soufflé I love. This corn recipe came to me from Mobile, Alabama.*

4 c. corn from 6 ears
1 c. fresh basil leaves, torn
3 T. all-purpose flour
1 tsp. sugar
¼ tsp. salt
4 large eggs, slightly beaten
1 c. milk
1 c. heavy cream

In a medium bowl, mix first five ingredients together (corn to salt.) In a separate bowl, mix the eggs, milk and cream. Then mix both bowls together. Bake at 350° for 45 min. to 1 hour until center is just set. Let rest 15 minutes. Serve immediately.

## Carolina Corn Salad

*I look forward to trying this recipe at our next cook-out here at the Governor's Mansion.*

1 T. cider vinegar
⅓ c. vegetable oil
2 T. fresh lemon juice
1 clove garlic, minced
1 tsp. dried parsley flakes
½ tsp. sugar
1 T. sweet pickle relish
Salt and pepper (to taste)
½ c. roasted red bell pepper, chopped
1 ½ c. canned whole kernel corn, drained
½ c. red onion, chopped

In small mixing bowl, combine vinegar, oil, lemon juice, garlic, parsley, sugar, pickle relish, salt and pepper. Set aside. In large mixing bowl, combine red bell pepper, corn and red onion. Pour dressing over salad mixture and toss lightly. Let stand a few minutes before serving.

# Corn Chowder

*This one is for all soup lovers! Nothing is better on cold rainy days than soup and cornbread.*

2 tsp. butter
½ c. onion, chopped
3 c. whole kernel corn
2 medium eggs, slightly beaten
1 c. celery, chopped
2 tsp. sugar
1 ½ tsp. salt
1 tsp. pepper
2 tsp. all-purpose flour
1 qt. milk, divided
1 c. crisp bacon pieces

In large skillet, combine butter, onion, corn, eggs, celery, sugar, salt and pepper. Cook over medium heat until vegetables are tender. Mix flour with ¼ c. of milk, stirring until smooth. Add to corn mixture. Stir in remaining milk. Add bacon pieces and cook over low heat until hot, stirring constantly. Do not boil.

Yield: 4 servings

# Country Corn Scallop

*I love casseroles and after the first 25 years of marriage, I finally talked Governor Riley into eating casseroles. This one is really good with most anything.*

¼ c. butter or margarine
⅓ c. all-purpose flour
¾ tsp. dry mustard
¼ tsp. paprika
½ tsp. salt
1 ⅓ c. scalded milk
20 oz. can cream style corn
1 medium egg, beaten
1 T. Worcestershire sauce
¾ c. buttered bread or cracker crumbs

In medium sauce pot, melt butter over medium-low heat. Stir in flour, mustard, paprika and salt. Gradually add milk, stirring constantly until mixture thickens. Add corn, egg and Worcestershire sauce. Pour into buttered 1 ½ quart casserole dish. Preheat oven at 325˚. Top with bread crumbs and bake for 30 minutes or until brown.

Yield: 6 servings

# Mama's Beef Chow Mein

*I love Chinese food and this recipe is one my family loves. My Mama made it when I was very young and even as a child I could not get enough. If you love Chow Mein, you'll enjoy this recipe. I hope it will become a favorite at your house.*

1 bottle soy sauce
1 ½ lbs. sirloin cubes
1 c. flour
¼ c. flour set aside
Salt and pepper to taste
¾ c. oil
2 cans LaChoy noodles
1 can LaChoy Chinese vegetables
1 can LaChoy bean sprouts
2 cans LaChoy bamboo shoots
2 cans LaChoy chopped water chestnuts
1 c. water

Toss sirloin cubes in flour. Heat oil and brown sirloin cubes. Add ½ c. soy sauce. Add to meat LIQUID ONLY from the following: canned vegetables, water chestnuts, bamboo shoots and bean sprouts. Stir well and cook for one hour on low heat. Add small amount of water to ¼ cup of flour to make paste. Add slowly and stir in to make a gravy type sauce. After meat and sauce cooks on low for 30 minutes, add vegetables, water chestnuts, bamboo shoots and bean sprouts to meat mixture. Heat well. Serve over toasted noodles. Add soy sauce to each serving if desired.

# Angel Biscuits

1 envelope active dry yeast
¼ c. warm water
2 ½ c. flour
2 T. sugar
1 tsp. salt
1 tsp. baking powder
½ tsp. baking soda
½ c. shortening
1 c. buttermilk

Dissolve the yeast in the warm water. Mix the flour, sugar, salt, baking powder and baking soda in a large bowl. Cut in the shortening until the mixture is crumbly. Add the buttermilk and the yeast mixture. Stir until a soft dough forms. Knead the dough on a lightly floured surface three to four times or until the dough is no longer sticky. Roll out the dough to a ½ inch thickness. Cut with a biscuit cutter. Place rounds on a greased baking sheet. Let rise for 15 to 30 minutes or until doubled in bulk. Preheat the oven to 400˚. Bake the biscuits for 12 to 15 minutes or until golden brown.

Yield: 1 dozen

# Herb-Crusted Salmon with Sun Dried Tomato Sauce

4 tsp. olive oil
2 T. minced shallots
1 T. fresh lemon juice, strained
½ c. dry white wine
6 sun dried tomatoes, rehydrated and minced
½ tsp. coarse salt
½ tsp. freshly ground black pepper
1 T. minced fresh basil
1 T. minced fresh thyme
2 tsp. minced fresh rosemary leaves
½ c. dry bread crumbs
2 (12 oz.) salmon fillets, skinned

In a 10 inch nonstick skillet, heat 2 teaspoons of the oil over medium heat. Add the shallots and sauté, stirring constantly, until lightly golden, about 1 minute. Add the lemon juice, wine and sun dried tomatoes. Increase the heat to medium high and cook until the sauce is reduced to ½ cup, about 2 minutes. Season with salt and pepper and set aside. (Sauce can be made up to 1 hour before cooking fish. Reheat over low heat, just before removing fish from the oven.)
Preheat the oven to 350˚. Lightly grease a 13 X 9 inch ovenproof baking dish with cooking spray. Set aside. On a piece of waxed paper, combine the basil, thyme, rosemary and bread crumbs. Dredge each fillet in the bread crumb mixture, coating well. Transfer the fillets to the prepared pan, placing them 2 inches apart.

Drizzle with the remaining 2 teaspoons of oil. Bake just until fish is opaque and barely flakes when tested in the center with a knife (about 8 to 10 minutes or more for thicker fillets). Transfer the fish to a serving platter. Cut each fillet crosswise in half, spoon sauce over fillets and serve.

Yield: 2 servings

# Easy Quiche

½ c. mayonnaise
2 T. flour
2 eggs, beaten
½ c. whole milk
1 ⅔ c. crabmeat, drained and flaked
8 oz. Swiss cheese, diced
⅓ c. sliced green onions
1 egg white, beaten
2 pie shells, unbaked or tiny pie shells for each lady

Combine the mayonnaise, flour, eggs and milk. Whisk until blended. Stir in the crabmeat, cheese and green onions. Preheat the oven to 350˚. Brush the pastry shells with egg white before filling to seal the crust and prevent sogginess. Pour the mixture into the pastry shells. Bake for 40 to 45 minutes.

*NOTE: You can use 1 cup of chopped ham instead of the crabmeat, if you prefer.*

Yield: 10-12 servings

# Italian Baked Eggplant

1 large eggplant
1 clove garlic, thinly sliced
¼ c. olive oil
1 large white onion, finely chopped
1 stalk celery, peeled, finely chopped
1 (15 oz.) can stewed tomatoes
1 T sugar
1 tsp. finely chopped fresh basil
Salt and pepper to taste
½ c. shredded sharp Cheddar cheese

Cut the eggplant lengthwise in half. Scoop out the pulp carefully, leaving the shells intact. Chop the pulp into ½ inch pieces. Preheat the oven to 375°. Sauté the garlic in the olive oil in a 12 inch skillet for 2 minutes. Add the eggplant pulp, onion and celery. Reduce the heat to medium. Sauté, stirring frequently for 10 minutes or until the vegetables are tender. Stir in the undrained tomatoes. Cook, stirring frequently, until thickened and most of the liquid has evaporated. Add the sugar, basil, salt and pepper. Mix well. Spoon the mixture into the eggplant shells and sprinkle with the cheese. Arrange the stuffed shells in a shallow baking dish. Pour in enough hot water to reach a depth of ½ inch around the shells. Bake for 20 to 30 minutes or until light brown.

Yield: 2 servings

# Noel Nut Ball Cookies

1 c. (2 sticks) butter, softened
½ c. confectioners' sugar
1 tsp. vanilla extract
2 ¼ c. flour
¼ tsp. salt
¾ c. chopped pecans

Preheat the oven to 400°. Cream the butter, confectioners' sugar and vanilla in a large bowl. Add the flour, salt and pecans to the butter mixture and mix. Chill the dough for approximately 30 minutes.
Roll the dough into 1 inch balls and place on an ungreased cookie sheet. Bake for 10 to 12 minutes, until lightly browned. While still warm, roll the balls in confectioners' sugar. Wait and roll them again to cover.

Yield: 4 dozen

# Hello Dollies

½ c. (1 stick) butter, melted
1 c. graham cracker crumbs
1 c. flaked coconut
1 c. chocolate bits
1 c. chopped pecans
1 can sweetened condensed milk

Preheat the oven to 350°. Mix the butter and crumbs and press firmly into a 9 inch square pan. Add a layer each of coconut, chocolate and nuts. Pour the milk over the top. Bake for 30 minutes. Cool in the pan. Cut into squares.

Yield: 16 servings

# Coolrise Orange Rolls

**Coolrise Sweet Dough:**
6-7 c. all-purpose flour
2 packages dry yeast
½ c. sugar
1 ½ tsp. salt
½ c. (1 stick) unsalted butter, at room temperature
1 ½ c. hot water
2 large eggs, at room temperature

**Orange Filling:**
3 c. sifted powdered sugar
1 T. grated orange zest
6 T. unsalted butter, at room temperature
¼ c. fresh orange juice

Combine 2 cups of the flour, the yeast, sugar and salt in a large bowl. Stir to blend. Add the butter and hot water all at once. Beat with a mixer at medium speed for 2 minutes, scraping the bowl occasionally. Add the eggs and 1 cup of the flour. Beat at high speed 1 minute, scraping the bowl occasionally. Gradually stir in enough of the remaining flour to make a soft dough that leaves the sides of the bowl. Turn the dough out onto a floured board and knead for 5 to 10 minutes. Cover loosely with plastic wrap, then a towel. Let the dough rest for 20 minutes on the board. Punch down. Combine the powdered sugar, orange zest, butter and orange juice in a large bowl. Divide the Coolrise Sweet Dough in half and roll each piece into a 14 X 7 inch rectangle. Spread each rectangle with one-fourth of the orange filling, leaving a 1 inch margin on the long sides. Roll the dough jelly-roll fashion, starting at a long side. Pinch seam to seal, but do not seal ends. Cut into 12 equal slices per roll. Place slices, cut side down, in greased muffin pans. Cover loosely with plastic wrap and place in refrigerator for 2 to 24 hours. Preheat the oven to 375˚. Bake the rolls for 15 to 20 minutes. Frost rolls with remaining orange filling while still warm, but not hot.

Yield: 2 dozen

# Reuben Dip

*Governor Riley loves Reubens anyway you can make them. This is a great way to enjoy a Reuben as a snack or appetizer.*

8 oz. cream cheese
8 oz. sour cream
½ lb. corned beef, crumbled
16 oz. can sauerkraut
1 T. caraway seed
½ lb. Swiss cheese, grated

In large mixing bowl, combine cream cheese, sour cream and corned beef. Mix well. Stir in sauerkraut, caraway seed and Swiss cheese. Pour into 9 x 13 inch baking dish and bake in preheated 350˚ oven for 30 minutes. Cool and serve with cocktail rye bread.

# Pecan Cheese Dip

*We are always looking for something different and easy to serve at the Alabama Governor's Mansion. This recipe keeps well for days and is very healthy served with carrot sticks or stuffed into celery sticks.*

> 2 (5 oz.) jars sharp Cheddar cheese
> 2 T. prepared mustard
> 1 c. toasted pecans, finely chopped
> 3 oz. package cream cheese
> 1 tsp. dry ranch salad dressing mix
> 2 T. Worcestershire sauce
> 1 tsp. paprika

In large mixing bowl, combine cheese, mustard, pecans, cream cheese, salad dressing mix and Worcestershire sauce. Mix well. When ready to serve, spread on crackers of your choice and sprinkle with paprika.

# Soooo Good! Deviled Eggs

*Once these are made, I have to hide them from certain family members or... we have a lot that go missing.*

> 12 large hard boiled eggs
> 2 ½ T. mayonnaise
> ¼ c. sweet pickle relish
> Salt and pepper to taste
> Paprika

Hard boil eggs and let cool. Remove shells from eggs. Rinse with cold water. Cut eggs in half lengthwise. Remove yolks. Place in medium size mixing bowl.

Mash with fork. Mix in mayonnaise and pickle relish. (Drain relish on a paper towel before adding to egg mixture.) Add salt and pepper to taste. Fill whites with egg mixture. Sprinkle tops with paprika.

# Double-Stuffed Eggs

*The potato flakes make a full-bodied filling, perfect for piping. One basic recipe makes three variations. Chill overnight.*

> 1 dozen hard cooked eggs, peeled
> ¾ c. light mayonnaise
> ½ c. instant potato flakes
> 1 T. Dijon mustard
> ¼ tsp. salt
> ¼ tsp. pepper
> Garnish: fresh dill sprigs

Cut eggs in half lengthwise. Remove yolks, leaving egg whites intact. Process egg yolks, mayonnaise and next 4 ingredients in a food processor until smooth, stopping to scrape down sides.
Spoon filling into egg whites. Cover and chill up to 8 hours. Garnish, if desired.

### Bacon-Stuffed Eggs
Stir ¾ c. (8 slices) crumbled cooked bacon, 3 T. pickle relish and ¼ c. chopped fresh chives into egg mixture. Proceed as directed.

### Shrimp-Stuffed Eggs
Stir ¼ pound fresh shrimp, cooked, peeled and chopped, 2 T. prepared horseradish and 6 minced green onions into egg mixture. Proceed as directed. Fill egg whites.

## Summer Fruit and Dip

*This is a great pool side dish for summer parties or weekends at the lake or beach with grandchildren. This is very refreshing on those hot southern summer days.*

8 oz. cream cheese
8 oz. jar marshmallow fluff
½ tsp. cinnamon
½ tsp. nutmeg

Fruit suggestions:
1 c. fresh peaches, chunks
2 bananas
1 c. fresh strawberries, halved
1 c. fresh pineapple, chunks
1 fresh orange, peeled and sliced
2 apples, cored and sliced

In a large mixing bowl, blend cream cheese and marshmallow fluff until creamy. Stir in cinnamon and nutmeg. Place fruit on serving platter with dip bowl. Pour cheese mixture in dip bowl and serve.

## Beef and Vegetable Stir Fry

*This recipe can be a healthy and fancy way to serve a nice dish that will please the palate.*

½ lb. flank steak
3 T. vegetable oil, divided
1 medium onion, sliced thin
2 c. vegetables, sliced thin**
¼ tsp. sugar
1 T. water
2 tsp. cornstarch
1 ½ tsp. soy sauce
1 tsp. fresh ginger, shredded

***Vegetables may include broccoli, cabbage, green bell pepper, cauliflower, zucchini, cucumber, mushrooms, water chestnuts and bamboo shoots, all sliced thin.*

Slice steak against grain. Cut in 2 inch strips approximately ½ inch thick. Preheat skillet or wok using 1 tablespoon vegetable oil. Add onion and your choice of vegetables. Stir-fry for 2 minutes, but do not allow vegetables to wilt or turn brown. In small mixing bowl, combine sugar, water, cornstarch and soy sauce. Add to beef mixture. Remove stir-fry and set aside. Preheat skillet or wok (again) and add remaining 2 tablespoons of vegetable oil. Add beef pieces and ginger. Stir fry until beef pieces separate and start to change color. Add cooked vegetables and stir to blend. Cook for 1 minute. Serve over rice or pasta.

Yield: 2-4 servings

# Crabmeat Salad

*Ladies, this one is a delight for summer luncheons or served in phyllo cups for an afternoon tea. I love to keep dips and salads in the refrigerator for drop by company or to serve at meetings I might have at the Governor's Mansion during the week.*

1 lb. fresh crabmeat, flaked
1 tsp. onion, grated
1 T. pimiento, minced
½ c. celery, minced
2 T. lemon juice
¼ tsp. salt
Mayonnaise to taste
Lettuce leaves
2 T. parsley, minced
Cucumber slices
Tomato slices

In large mixing bowl, combine crabmeat, onion, pimiento and celery. Sprinkle with lemon juice, add salt and toss to mix. Add a small amount of mayonnaise (just enough to moisten) and mix well. Arrange lettuce on serving plate and spoon crabmeat mixture onto lettuce. Sprinkle lightly with parsley, garnish dish with thin slices of cucumber and tomato slices.

Yield: 4 servings

# Fresh Crab Bisque

*I love soups and bisque year round. This one is great to whip up at the beach when you can get fresh seafood.*

1 lb. crabmeat
¼ c. butter, melted
2 T. onion, chopped
2 T. celery, chopped
3 T. all-purpose flour

1 tsp. salt
⅛ tsp. white pepper
¼ tsp. paprika
1 qt. milk or half & half
¼ c. parsley, chopped

Remove remaining shell or cartridge from crabmeat. In large sauce pot, add butter. Sauté onion and celery until tender. Do not brown. Blend in flour. Add salt, pepper and paprika. While cooking over low heat, gradually add milk, stirring constantly. Cook until mixture thickens. Add crabmeat and cook until thoroughly heated. Sprinkle with parsley when served.

Yield: 6 servings

# Spicy Shrimp and Corn Soup

½ c. green onions, chopped
1 medium onion, chopped
2 T. margarine
2 (11 oz.) cans cream style corn
2 (10 ¾ oz.) cans cream of potato soup
1 c. water
1 ½ caps liquid shrimp/crab boil
1 ½ lbs. shrimp, peeled and deveined
Salt and pepper (to taste)

In heavy sauce pot, sauté all onions in margarine until translucent. Add corn, potato soup, water and liquid shrimp/ crab boil. Bring to a boil over medium heat, adding more water if needed. Add shrimp, cook until shrimp are just tender. Add salt and pepper to taste. Reduce heat and simmer until ready to serve.

Yield: 4-5 servings

# Oyster Stew

½ c. butter or margarine
2 pt. fresh oysters
4 c. milk
1 c. light cream
Salt and pepper to taste
Hot sauce to taste, optional

In medium size heavy skillet, melt butter or margarine and add oysters (with liquid). Cook over low heat until edges of oysters begin to curl. Set aside. In large sauce pot, add milk and cream, stirring while gradually heating. Stir in oysters, salt and pepper to taste. Add hot sauce if desired. Cover and simmer over low heat until ready to serve.

Yield: 6-8 servings

# Shrimp Puffs

*In the early 1900s, Samuel B. Thomas used his mother's teacake recipe and created the English muffin. This is a wonderful way to use the English muffin. For many Alabama shrimpers, making a living from the gulf is a proud family heritage. Traditional values of long days of hard honest labor have been handed down from one generation to the next.*

8 oz. cream cheese
½ c. mayonnaise
1 T. onion flakes
½ c. Parmesan cheese, grated
Dash garlic
6 oz. can shrimp
12 oz. package English muffins

In a large mixing bowl, mix cream cheese, mayonnaise, onion flake, Parmesan cheese and dash of garlic. Add shrimp to mix. Split English muffins. Spread shrimp mixture on halves and bake at 375° until golden brown.

# Shrimp Bisque

*I make this at the beach each summer and I learned quickly one recipe was not enough. My family loves this one.*

1 (10 ¾ oz.) can condensed cream of mushroom soup
1 (10 ¾ oz.) can condensed cream of chicken soup
2 (12 oz.) cans evaporated milk
2 T. butter
½ lb. cooked shrimp, peeled, deveined and chopped
Dash of Worcestershire sauce
Dash of Tabasco
¼ to ½ c. sherry or to taste

In top of double boiler, heat soups, milk and butter over boiling water. Add shrimp, Worcestershire sauce and Tabasco. Stir in sherry to taste. Continue heating until desired temperature. Great served plain or over steamed rice.

# Family and Friends' Favorites

# Notes

# Family and Friends' Favorites

It's been quite a journey for Bob and me the past 60 plus years. Most of our days on this journey have been happy ones. With loving family and supportive friends, each road we've taken has been a great adventure.

These next recipes come from family, extended family and friends God has brought into our lives for which we are so grateful!

I've served each one of these to guests and family. I have loved being able to ring the dinner bell for these great dishes.

## Hot Beef Dip

*Every time I prepare this wonderful dip, I have a sweet visit with the past. I also have a sweet visit with two wonderful ladies, Jenice Riley and Judy Jackson of Birmingham, Alabama. Years ago we were visiting with Gary and Judy when she came out with this rich creamy beef dip. Jenice and Bob could make a meal out of this dish. So every time I make it, I have a visit with God, also. I thank Him in silence for all my blessings of friends and memories of our daughter who now lives in Heaven.*

> 2 pkgs. (8 oz.) cream cheese, softened
> 1 (8 oz.) carton sour cream
> 2 T. milk
> 4 T. minced bell pepper
> 4 T. onion, minced
> 1 pkg. dried beef, chopped finely
> ½ c. chopped nuts

Mix all ingredients. Bake 20 minutes at 350˚. Serve with Wheat Thins. Freezes well.

*Tip: If it gets dry, add a tiny bit of milk.*

## Miss Patsy's Watermelon Salad with Poppy Seed Dressing

*In the good ole' summertime, I like to cool things off with a big watermelon salad. It's very healthy.*

> 1 sm. red watermelon, cut into seedless balls
> 1 carton fresh pineapple, cut into cubes
> 1 fresh cantaloupe, cut into balls
> 1 honeydew melon, cut into balls
> 1 carton fresh strawberries, sliced
> 2 bananas, sliced
> 1 red apple, chopped
> 1 green apple, chopped
> 1 c. raisins
> 2 fresh peaches, sliced
> White and Red Grapes
> and any other favorite fruit of your choice.

Toss well after all fruits have been sliced, chopped and shaped into balls. Place in large bowl. Place watermelon salad in serving bowls or open faced watermelon rind, if you have that artistic flair.

# Simply the Best Poppy Seed Dressing

½ c. sugar
½ c. vinegar
1 c. Wesson oil
1 T. poppy seeds
1 tsp. dry mustard
1 tsp. salt
1 tsp. onion juice

Beat sugar, vinegar and oil. Add mustard, salt and onion juice. Beat again. Add poppy seeds and beat again. This is great over fruit salad or watermelon salad in the summertime. Place salad in bowls and pour dressing over salad or place bowl of dressing on the table. Let your guests pour away!

# Cinnamon Swirls at the Pirkle's House

*These cinnamon swirls will be so good to crunch on as we sit by a nice fire and share our day. Or what a delight to bring in the new day with these swirls for breakfast. Rick Pirkle, my nephew-in-law, would probably enjoy a fruit plate with our cinnamon swirls. It's so nice when you enjoy, really enjoy your family members. Rick and I love to laugh over the silliest things!*

1 loaf of bread
1 pkg. (8 oz.) of cream cheese, softened
½ c. sugar
1 egg yolk

Trim edges of bread and flatten slices. Cream together. Spread cream cheese mixture onto one side of bread. Roll up slices of bread. Dip in melted butter. Roll in cinnamon sugar:

1 T. cinnamon
1 c. sugar

Freeze rolls 2-3 hours (up to 6 months). Cut into thirds. Bake at 400° for 10 minutes. Serve warm.

# Delightful Banana-Cherry Salad

*Summertime is a great time to try this one. I love it! So...easy!*

2 pkgs. cherry Jell-O
2 bananas
1 (16 oz.) carton sour cream
1 pkg. small marshmallows
1 c. pecans, coarsely chopped

Mix Jell-O as directed. Let thicken to egg white consistency. Slice bananas and add to thickened Jell-O. Pour into 9x13 inch casserole dish. Place back in refrigerator until it is very firm. In a bowl, mix together sour cream and marshmallows, just fold gently until marshmallows are coated with sour cream. Spread evenly over very firm Jell-O. Be gentle as not to cut into Jell-O. Sprinkle coarsely chopped pecans on top of marshmallow topping. Place back in refrigerator for at least 30 minutes. Cut into squares and serve on lettuce bed.

# Ruthie's Favorite Asparagus and English Pea Casserole

*From one generation to the next, this recipe is a family and friends' favorite. Our niece, Ruthie, enjoys preparing this one that was passed down from her mother, Sara and Mama Verna, my mother and her grandmother. She is the only member of the family who followed in Daddy's footsteps and became a pharmacist. We knew very early on in her life what plans she had in her mind, when at 3 years old she told us she wanted to be a pharmacist just like Daddy John.*

1 (12 oz.) can green tip asparagus
1 (15 oz.) can Leseur English peas
3 c. white sauce "thick"
4 hard-boiled eggs
1 (4 oz.) cream cheese
Cracker crumbs

Drain peas well. Drain asparagus and set liquid aside. Add asparagus liquid to white sauce. Dissolve cream cheese in white sauce while hot. Spray casserole dish and layer asparagus, peas, sliced boiled eggs and white sauce. Add cracker crumbs a few minutes before removing from oven (optional). Bake at 350˚ for 30 minutes.

Basic White Sauce:
4 T. butter
4 T. flour
½ tsp. salt
Dash pepper
2 c. milk or half & half

Melt butter on low heat. Add flour slowly. Stir until blended. Add salt and pepper. Slowly add milk, stir until smooth. Add more milk for thin sauce and less for thick sauce.

# Gale's Fabulous Chicken Casserole

*This recipe comes from a dear friend from our Ashland childhood. We were in grade school and high school together. I was in her wedding in February after Rob was born in December. This friend was a prayer warrior during Jenice's fight with cancer. We had babies together and now grandbabies together. She has given time and love to me through the years, but the best thing she has given Bob and me lately is Jim, her husband, who is our State's Financial Director. Thanks, Gale Main, I love this recipe. Remember 30 years ago when you brought this casserole to the lake?*

2 c. chicken chopped
4 c. white rice
1 c. celery
2 T. onion
1 c. water chestnuts, sliced
1 c. cream of chicken soup
¾ c. mayo
1 c. mushrooms, sliced and drained

Mix all ingredients and put in a casserole dish. It should be very creamy. Cook at 350˚ until bubbly. Top with croutons then toast. Serve when croutons are golden brown.

*I usually serve a cranberry salad with this great and easy casserole.*

# Mama's Old Time Ice Box Rolls

*While cleaning out my parents' house of 65 years, I found Mama's handwritten cookbook. Many of the names by the recipes are ladies I remember from my childhood and I remember their visits to our home. What wonderful old recipes and wonderful old friends! I want to share two with you. These have to be about 60 years old. I took this right out of Mama's cookbook, word for word. I can hear her voice so clearly as I'm writing...*

Combine 1 yeast cake, 1 tsp. sugar, ¼ c. lukewarm water and let stand until needed. Pour 1 c. boiling water over 3 T. sugar, 1 tsp. salt and 4 T. shortening. Allow to cool until lukewarm. Add one egg, slightly beaten. Add yeast mixture. Add 2 c. flour and beat until smooth. Add another 2 to 2 ½ c. flour. Place in icebox over night or all day. Make into rolls of any desired shape. Brush with butter and place in greased pans. Allow to rise 1 ½ to 2 hours. Bake in "quick" oven 425° for 12 to 15 minutes.

# Divinity Cake

*This is another recipe in Mama's Cookbook. I remember eating this cake as a little girl. It's, also, one of the Governor's favorite cakes.*

> 1 c. shortening
> 2 c. sugar
> 3 c. sifted cake flour
> 3 tsp. baking powder
> Dash salt
> 1 c. milk
> 7 egg whites
> 1 tsp. vanilla

Cream shortening and sugar. Mix and sift flour, baking powder and salt. Add to first mixture alternately with milk. Fold in egg whites, beat until stiff, but not dry. Add vanilla. Turn into 2 greased 9 inch cake pans. Bake 375° for 25 minutes. Cool and frost.

# Divinity Frosting

> 1 c. sugar
> Pinch of cream of tartar
> ½ c. water
> 2 egg whites
> 1 tsp. vanilla
> ¼ c. chopped maraschino cherries
> ¼ c. chopped pecans

Combine sugar, cream of tartar and water. Cook to hard ball stage or 242° on a candy thermometer. Beat egg whites until stiff, but not dry. Very slowly, pour syrup over egg whites, beating constantly until very thick. Fold in vanilla, cherries and pecans. Frost cake.

# Cheesy Shrimp on Grits Toast

*These sound like so much fun to make. I'm planning to serve these this year at our annual Jenice Riley Memorial Kid One Luncheon. Kid One is a wonderful transport team that helps children get medical care. These little ones would not be able to get to a doctor or have the chemo and other treatments needed without Kid One. Each year, we have a luncheon to raise money for Kid One Transport. The guests will love these little toasts!*

3 (14 oz.) cans chicken broth
1 ⅓ c. quick-cooking grits
½ c. grated Parmesan
½ tsp. salt
2 T. butter, melted
8 oz. package cream cheese, softened
1 T. half & half
½ c. grated Italian cheese blend
1 tsp. chopped parsley leaves
½ lb. cooked, peeled, and deveined shrimp, chopped
½ c. grated Cheddar cheese

Preheat oven to 400°. Bring broth to a boil in a large saucepan. Stir in grits and return to a boil. Cover, reduce heat and simmer 5 minutes, or until grits are thickened, stirring occasionally. Stir in cheese and salt. Remove from heat. Spoon grits into a greased 9 by 13 inch baking pan. Cover and chill at least 2 hours or until firm. Unmold grits onto a large cutting board. Cut out 48 (1 ½ inch) circles using a round or fluted cookie cutter. Brush a large pan with melted butter. Place grit rounds on pan. Bake for 15 minutes. Turn grits and bake 45 minutes more. Set aside. (Up to this point, the recipe can be prepared ahead. If preparing early, cover and refrigerate grit rounds until you are ready to top with shrimp mixture.)
In a large bowl, combine cream cheese and half & half, stirring until combined. Stir in cheese, parsley and shrimp. Top each grits round evenly with shrimp mixture. Top mixture with grated Cheddar. Broil 5 minutes or until lightly browned and heated through.

# Krispy Kreme Bread Pudding with Butter Rum Sauce

*This one could get us in trouble. You know a moment on the lips, a lifetime on the hips!!!*

2 dozen Krispy Kreme donuts
1 (14 oz.) can sweetened condensed milk
2 (4 ½ oz.) cans fruit cocktail, undrained
2 eggs, beaten
1 (9 oz.) box raisins
1 pinch salt
1 or 2 tsp. ground cinnamon
Butter Rum Sauce, recipe follows

Preheat oven to 350˚. Cube donuts into a large bowl. Pour other ingredients on top of donuts and let soak for a few minutes. Mix all ingredients together until donuts have soaked up the liquid as much as possible. Bake for about 1 hour until center has jelled. Top with Butter Rum Sauce.

Butter Rum Sauce:
1 stick butter
1 lb. box confectioners' sugar
Rum, to taste

Melt butter and slowly stir in confectioners' sugar. Add rum and heat until bubbly. Pour over each serving of Krispy Kreme Bread Pudding.

# Seafood Lasagna

*One Saturday morning, Paula Deen was on TV. She was cooking Seafood Lasagna. I couldn't take time to write it down, but I knew Bob would love it. I prepared what I could remember on Sunday night and we really loved it. This is a little different from Paula's. I'm sure she'd say, "Go for it, girl!" If you like seafood, you'll add this one to your favorite list! This is coming right out of my head, so here it goes...*

½ box lasagna, cooked
½ stick butter
Dash of salt
Dash of pepper
4 to 6 T. flour - I use gravy and sauce flour by Pillsbury or Shake & Blend
2 c. half & half
1 clove garlic, chopped
½ c. chopped onions
1 (8 oz.) block of Swiss cheese
½ c. white cooking wine
Romano cheese
1 pkg. or 2 c. Cheddar and Monterey Jack cheese, shredded, for topping
10-12 large shrimp, uncooked, but peeled
2 cans crabmeat
12 scallops

Make white sauce (see page 89). Melt butter on low heat. Add flour, salt and pepper. Pour in half & half slowly. Stir until it thickens. Add onion and garlic. Keep on low heat. Cut Swiss cheese into cubes and add to white sauce or add 1 pkg. shredded Swiss cheese. Add ½ c. cooking sherry. Then add seafood. Cook until shrimp turns pink, take off heat. Spray a 9x13 inch casserole dish with oil. Then cover bottom with thin coat of white sauce. Layer with lasagna, then seafood white sauce mixture. Layer until white sauce is last. Top with Romano cheese, 2 c. Cheddar and Monterrey Jack. Bake at 350˚ until it bubbles and cheese turns lightly brown... Fabulous!

# Darby's Texas Hash

*Both our daughters have truly been blessed among women, as they both have wonderfully kind and loving mothers-in-law. These next two recipes come from JoAnne Crye and Darby Campbell. I love your sons as if they were my own boys. When you are watching your children grow up, both sons and daughters, you always wonder what kind of mates they will choose. I knew who they came in the back door with for keeps, would one day affect all of our lives. I, also, hoped my children would be blessed with kind, caring in-laws. Mothers and mothers-in-law set the tone when you enter the home. You know, "If Mama ain't happy, ain't nobody happy!" All of our children are blessed because they all have mothers-in-law who truly love them – and like them! Darby is close in heart, but far in distance. She lives in St. Petersburg, Florida. This is an old family recipe from our son-in-law's grandmother, Josephine, This is Rob Campbell's favorite dish. His mom loves to prepare it for him.*

> 1 lb. or more lean ground meat
> 2 large yellow onions
> 2 large green peppers or a half can of sweet pepper flakes
> 1 ½ cloves of garlic, press in garlic press
> 1 tsp. salt
> 1 tsp. chili powder
> ¾ c. rice
> 1 large can (28 oz.) tomato puree
> 1 can (10 ¾ oz.) tomato puree

Preheat oven to 375˚. Brown meat in butter or margarine until it falls apart. Brown onions and green peppers together in another pan while the meat is browning. To covered 3 qt. casserole, add the two cans of puree, salt, rice, chili powder and garlic. Drain any of the butter or margarine from the pans used for browning. Then add the browned meat, onions and peppers to the casserole. Mix it all well. Cover the casserole. Place it in oven at 375˚ for 45-60 minutes. Test rice at 45 minutes. When rice is soft, casserole is done. Turn oven off and take out of oven. It can burn quickly.

# JoAnne Crye's Shrimp Ball

*When Bob and I think of great supporters, we think of Pete and JoAnne Crye of Irondale. They are wonderful in-laws to our daughter Krisalyn and grandparents to Madilyn Jenice, our granddaughter. We all miss Joanne, but take comfort in the sweet memories we shared with her while she was here with us on earth. I dedicate this great recipe to JoAnne Crye.*

> 16 oz. cream cheese
> ½ tsp. pepper
> 2 T. Ketchup
> 1 tsp. minced onion
> ½ tsp. Cayenne pepper
> 1 T. Worcestershire sauce
> ½ tsp. Tabasco sauce
> 10 oz. small shrimp, deveined

Mix all ingredients together well and form into a ball. Chill several hours and serve with crackers.

# Walter's Wild Duck Appetizer

*Both Walter Crye and Rob Campbell, our sons-in-law, love to hunt. They have worked so very hard on our farm and the hunting areas on the farm. I guess I'd be safe to say they enjoy every kind of hunting. It's wonderful that they enjoy spending time together. Walter and Krisalyn, also, enjoy duck hunting and both have beautiful stuffed ducks from a trip to Arkansas. While they were on this hunting trip, Walter discovered this great appetizer.*

>       Duck breasts
>       Italian salad dressing
>       Cream cheese
>       Jalapeño peppers
>       Bacon
>       Toothpicks
>       Cajun seasoning

Remove the duck breasts and marinate in Italian dressing overnight. Cut a pocket into each breast and stuff the breasts with cream cheese and jalapeño peppers. Wrap tightly in bacon and secure with toothpicks. Grill until bacon is done and breast meat is medium at most. (Cajun seasoning is a great addition while grilling.) Remove from grill and slice into bite size pieces. Serve hot as a delicious appetizer at the hunting club.

# Rob Campbell's Best Steak Pennington

*It's so nice to watch our children and their families come home to Ashland and enjoy the woods and all the activities that go along with living in the country. Our son-in-law, Rob, grew up in St. Petersburg, Florida. I wasn't sure if he would like the country roads that would bring them home. He loves everything about the country! He loves to cook for all of us when we get home together. We are blessed by both our sons-in-law. They always make us feel welcome at their homes in Birmingham and are always there when we need them.*

>       Steaks of your choice
>       Stubbs Beef Marinade
>       Garlic, pepper or steak season-
>       ing of choice
>       1 c. Dale's marinade
>       ⅔ c. bourbon of choice
>       1 tsp. sugar
>       3 T. favorite steak sauce
>       1 stick of butter

Marinate steaks in Stubbs beef marinade for 1 hour at room temperature. Season with garlic, pepper or steak seasoning before grilling. At the same time you put the steaks on the grill, put the Dale's, bourbon, sugar, favorite steak sauce and butter in a baking dish. Place in a preheated 400° oven. When you take the steaks off the grill, place them in the mixture. Leave them there one minute. Spoon a little more over each steak as you serve them. Keep an eye on the liquid in the oven and if it starts cooking down too much, add a bit of water.

# Minda's Créme Brulee French Toast

*There are people in your life you can't get along without. That's our daughter Minda. She is a wonderful asset to our work and our family. She is a wonderful young mother. The little people in Minda and Rob's life right now are Bobby and Riley Jenice Campbell. Life is the first gift to baby Riley and Bobby, love is the second, and understanding is the third. They are so blessed. Minda always loves and understands them, but she is a master at laughing with them. Minda and Rob have learned the secret! Thanks, Minda for keeping us all laughing.*

1 ½ sticks butter
1 c. packed brown sugar
3 T. maple syrup, plus additional syrup to serve
½ tsp. rum extract
1 country-style loaf bread or 8-9 inch round of Brioche
6 eggs
1 ¾ c. half & half
1 tsp. vanilla extract
2 tsp. Grand Marnier
¼ tsp. salt
Powdered sugar
Cinnamon to taste (optional)

Butter a 9 x 13 baking dish. In a small saucepan over low heat, melt the butter with the sugar, maple syrup and rum extract. Pour the mixture into the dish. Cut six 1 ½ inch thick slices from the center of the bread. Arrange the bread in one layer in the baking dish, squeezing them slightly so they fit. In a bowl, whisk the eggs, half & half, vanilla, Grand Marnier and salt. Pour the mixture evenly over the bread. Cover with plastic wrap and chill at least 8 hours and up to one day. When ready to cook, remove the dish from the refrigerator and let it come to room temperature, about 30 minutes. Cook uncovered about 30 to 45 minutes at 350° or until puffed and golden brown. Sprinkle with powdered sugar and serve immediately with warm maple syrup.

# Mildred Williams Pound Cake

*When I first got married 44 years ago, I was told every homemaker needs a good pound cake recipe to take to sick folks and covered dish suppers at the church. Here is my old standby. Mildred was a dear friend of my Mama's and she was our florist when we married in 1964.*

1 c. Crisco
3 c. sugar
6 eggs
3 c. plain flour
½ pt. whipping cream
1 tsp. vanilla

Cream Crisco and 1 c. sugar. Alternate second and third cups of sugar with the six eggs. Beat well after each egg. Alternate flour and whipping cream. Add vanilla. Beat 2 to 3 minutes after the whipping cream and flour have been added. Fold into a heavily sprayed bundt pan for baking. Bake one hour at 350°. Let cool in pan for 10 minutes before turning out.

## Krisalyn's Chicken Dinner

*Krisalyn and Walter added a new family member on July 29, 2006. We have our seventh grandchild, little Madilyn Jenice. They both make wonderful parents. It seems like such a long wait to hold, touch and look at that beautiful face. And now, through Kris and Walter's eyes, this little one will be introduced to sounds and sights of our world. It takes two large hands to show two tiny ones how to clap, wave goodbye, throw a kiss and buckle up for safety. Bob and I are so blessed to be close enough to share in all the joy of this first baby! When this baby laughed for the first time, the laugh broke into a thousand pieces and they all went skipping about, and that was the beginning of fairies! That's what Madi reminds me of these days, a tiny fairy.*

**1 lb. fresh broccoli, cooked and drained**
**3 chicken breasts, cooked and chopped**
**1 can broccoli and cheese soup**
**⅓ c. milk**
**½ c. cheese, shredded**
**4 T. dry breadcrumbs**
**1 T. butter**

Place broccoli and chopped chicken in casserole dish. Mix soup and milk. Pour over chicken and broccoli. Sprinkle cheese on top. Mix bread crumbs and butter. Add to top. Bake at 450˚ for 20 minutes. If you'd like a vegetarian dinner, substitute cauliflower for chicken.

## Miss Peggy's Birthday Cake & Divinity Icing

*Jubilation! That was my thought when I heard 'Miss Peggy Waites' would share my favorite birthday cake recipe with me! She started making my birthday cakes for my Mama when I was about 8 years old. The cake, an angel food cake, would be the skirt for a beautiful doll in the center. Of course, Miss Peggy decorated the cake to make it seem like the most gorgeous dress... fit for Cinderella! Every year, through my teens, after I married, during my child-bearing years, and throughout all my birthdays, Miss Peggy came to my door with a pink cake. I can see, smell and taste it right now. I am so honored Miss Peggy gave me the recipe because my daughters all began to ask for the same birthday cake every year. Now, maybe I can learn to ice their special cakes year after year.*
*Thanks, Miss Peggy, for the memories!*

**1 ¾ c. sugar**
**1 tsp. vanilla flavoring**
**½ c. hot water**
**1 T. white Karo syrup**
**Pinch of salt**

Mix all above ingredients. Stir well and bring to a boil until it spins a long thread.

**3 egg whites**
**1 tsp. powdered sugar**

Take 3 egg whites and beat until stiff. Add 1 tsp. powdered sugar and beat. Slowly add syrup mixture. Beat until fluffy. It should not have a shine. Does not do well in rainy weather.

# Elizabeth Riley's Red Velvet Cake

*Bob's mother baked the best Red Velvet cakes. When Sue, my sister-in-law, and I cleaned out their house, I looked and looked for her recipe book, but I never found it. While writing this cookbook, I found her cake recipe with my Mama's cookbook. The recipe is in Bob's mother's handwriting so it's priceless to me. I hope these recipes will be a treasure for my daughters and granddaughters. I remember her making this cake at Christmas time right after Bob and I were married. I'm so glad I finally found this wonderful cake.*

½ c. Crisco
1 ½ c. sugar
2 eggs
1 tsp. salt
2 ¼ c. flour
1 tsp. soda
¼ c. red food color (2 bottles)
3 tsp. vanilla
2 tsp. cocoa
1 c. buttermilk
1 tsp. vinegar

Cream Crisco and sugar. Add eggs and beat. Put in cocoa. Add vanilla and make a paste. Add salt, soda and 2 tsp. vanilla. Add to milk. Then alternate, adding milk and flour. Before adding all the milk, add vinegar and blend in cake coloring. Bake in 2 layers at 350° for about 25-30 minutes.

Frosting:
1 c. milk
5 tsp. flour
2 sticks of oleo
1 c. powdered sugar
1 tsp. vanilla
1 c. nuts

Cook milk and flour over low heat, stirring until thick. Place in refrigerator to cool. Cream 2 sticks oleo. Add 1 c. powdered sugar, sifted. Add 1 tsp. vanilla. Beat with mixer. Add flour mixture. Add nuts and frost cake.

# She Crab Soup

*A friend is someone who loves you on your best days and loves you through your worst days. That's my friend Bonnie Williams. Her She Crab Soup is wonderful.*

2 T. butter
1 T. flour
1 qt. milk
2 c. white crabmeat
5 drops onion juice
¼ tsp. pepper
¼ tsp. mace
½ tsp. salt
¼ pt. heavy cream, whipped
4-5 T. dry sherry
Grated grind of one lemon

In the top of a double boiler, melt butter and blend with flour until smooth. While stirring constantly, add the milk slowly. Then add the crabmeat and all the seasonings except the sherry. Cook over low heat for 20 minutes. Serve in warm cups with one teaspoon of sherry and a topping of whipped cream.

# Sunday Lunch Chicken at Phyllis Hoffman's House

*I remember the first time I picked up a* Southern Lady Magazine. *I knew I was hooked on this treasure for life or as long as I can get my hands on one! I never dreamed I'd meet the publisher... ever. I've been uniquely blessed to meet many people these past few years that I never dreamed I'd meet. Phyllis Hoffman is such a delight, fun to be with, so talented and plays the piano like an angel. There is not much this gal can't do! But the icing on her cake of life is she knows our Lord and she shares Him. She gives Him all the credit for life and successes! Thanks Phyllis, for all you do to bring beauty into all of our lives!*

> 6-8 boneless, skinless chicken breasts
> 1 can cream of chicken soup
> 1 can cream of mushroom soup
> 1 can cream of celery soup
> 1 c. uncooked rice
> 2 c. water
> ½ stick butter, melted
> Paprika

Preheat oven to 325°. Grease a 13 x 9 inch casserole dish. Mix soups, rice, water and butter together. Pour into dish. Place the chicken on top of the rice mixture, submerging it slightly. Sprinkle the chicken with paprika. Bake for 1 to 1 ½ hours until chicken is done and tender.

# Donna's Old-Fashioned Chicken and Dressing

*There is a voice in our world and once you've heard the "heart song" of the voice you'll never forget it. But it's much more than the voice you'll never forget, you'll never forget the smile, the words of wisdom and oh, the eyes. You'll never forget the eyes that go to the soul. Do not have your concert first and tune your instruments (voices) afterwards. Begin the day with God. I hear it in the voice that God is the beginning and the end of the day for Donna Allen, the voice from God!*

*This is a never-fail, moist recipe that EVERYONE loves and asks for more!*

> 1 c. self-rising corn meal
> 1 c. plain flour
> 2 eggs
> 3 tsp. baking powder
> 1 tsp. salt
> 1 ¼ c. sweet milk
> ¼ c. oil

Mix all ingredients. Bake at 500° until brown.

> 1 whole chicken cooked in 6 c. water
> 1 can cream of chicken soup
> 1 can cream of celery soup
> 2 medium onions
> 3 eggs
> 1 stick of margarine

Cook chicken until tender and remove bones. Bake bread. Mix with all ingredients. Bake at 350° until done.

# Savannah Low Country Boil

*This one is not only wonderful to eat, but it's fun to cook. Then dump out on brown paper and enjoy! This meal brings back memories of my cousin Kacie's wedding in 2005, as we gathered our family together a few nights before the wedding day. What a wonderful memory!*

5 lbs. shrimp (unpeeled and heads off)
2 dozen blue crabs, whole
20 or so small new potatoes
3 lbs. smoked sausage (cut into 2 inch pieces)
6 small Vidalia onions
8-10 cobs of corn (broken into 4 inch pieces)
2-3 lemons cut in half
Seafood seasoning (1 package of seafood boil)

In a big pot of boiling water, cook potatoes and seafood boil. Boil about ten minutes. Add crabs and onions. Cook another ten minutes. Add sausage, corn and shrimp and cook ten minutes more. Drain and dump onto a table covered with butcher paper or newspapers (or you can dump onto a large tray). Serve lemons on side.

# Mary Glenn's Chicken Wiggle

*Laughter puts the wrinkles in all the right places. You can't be around Mary Glenn without laughing because she is so "up" on life and she finds something to laugh about, no matter what. Jenice could call on this great friend at the midnight hour and she'd be there for our daughter.*

*Usually what Jenice needed took Mary Glenn into the midnight and later. I'm so thankful God has chosen Mary Glenn to be here for us during our days of being separated from Jenice for just a little while.*

*She got this recipe from her mother back in the early 70's when she and her husband Buddy were dating. She knew men raved about this dish and she wanted a "sure-fire way" to Buddy's heart... through his stomach! It must have worked. They've been married for 30 years!*

6-8 boneless chicken breasts
1 large jar of mushrooms
1 diced onion
1 (15 oz.) can tomatoes
salt
pepper
paprika
2 cans cream of mushroom soup
1 lb. grated cheese
12 oz. cooked flat egg noodles

Boil 6-8 boneless chicken breast halves until tender. Remove from water and cut into pieces. Put in a large pot and add 1 large jar of mushrooms, 1 diced onion, 1 (15 oz.) can of tomatoes, salt, pepper and paprika. Cook on low until seasoning gets into meat. Add 2 cans of cream of mushroom soup. Just before serving, add 1 lb. of grated Cheddar cheese and a 12 oz. package of cooked flat egg noodles. Yum!

# Mary Gaither's Indian Corn Stew

*I know this will be a family favorite! The Gaither-Pruet families have been a part of our lives even before Bob and I were ever born. I guess you could say this is our oldest friendship recipe. Thanks Mary, for teaching Kim, our previous special events coordinator, all her neat tricks for giving tours and special events with ease.*

1 lb. ground beef
1 medium onion, chopped
½ bell pepper, chopped
1 can whole tomatoes
1 can shoe peg corn
1 can tomato soup
2 tsp. sugar
1 tsp. salt
2 T. flour
2 T. water

Brown and drain ground beef. In blender, blend onion, bell pepper and whole tomatoes. Add blended vegetables, shoe peg corn, soup, sugar and salt to the ground beef. Simmer for 15 minutes. In separate bowl, mix flour and water. Stir into soup mixture. If too thick, add a little more water.

# The Bright Star Restaurant's Pineapple Cream Cheese Pie

*The Bright Star Restaurant in Bessemer comes by its name correctly, as it's a very bright star in the state of Alabama's history of restaurants. We are blessed to have been given this recipe by the owners Jim and Nick Koikos.*

1 (9 inch) deep-dish frozen pie shell, thawed
1 c. cool water
¼ c. cornstarch
2 (8 oz.) cans crushed pineapple, in juice
1 ¼ c. plus 2 T. sugar, divided
1 (8 oz.) package cream cheese, softened
¼ c. all-purpose flour
2 tsp. vanilla extract
1 egg
⅛ tsp. yellow food coloring
⅓ c. chopped almonds

Bake pie shell according to package directions until lightly brown. Remove from oven and allow to cool. Preheat oven to 325°.
In a small bowl, combine water and cornstarch, stirring until smooth and set aside.
In a small saucepan, combine pineapple and ¾ cup of sugar. Bring to a boil over medium-high heat on stovetop, stirring occasionally. Reduce heat to medium. Stir in cornstarch mixture and bring to a boil, stirring constantly for approximately 5 minutes. Remove from heat and let stand for 15 minutes.
In a mixing bowl, beat cream cheese, remaining ½ cup plus 2 tablespoons of sugar and flour at medium speed with an electric mixer until creamy. Add vanilla, egg and yellow food coloring, stirring until smooth. Add pineapple mixture to cream cheese mixture and mix until combined. Pour mixture into cooled pie shell. Top with almonds.
Bake for 30 minutes or until a tester inserted near center comes out clean. Allow to cool on a wire rack for 1 hour before serving. Serve warm or chilled.

Yield: A 9 inch deep dish pie

# Miss Prissy's
## Bits of Brittle Cookies

*I'll never forget my first visit to the Ruby Begonia in Homewood, Alabama. Jenice, our daughter, was so happy to be back in Alabama from her teaching days in Atlanta. One day, I was in Birmingham, and she wanted me to meet her new friend Prissy. "She's the most fun, Mom. You'll love her and she's been so nice to me. And you'll love her silver jewelry!" Jenice was right, but she never realized how close Prissy and I would become after she went to be with the Lord. She loved Prissy and Prissy loved and adored Jenice. Now we laugh and cry together remembering our special friend, Jenice. Prissy got this recipe from her mom several years ago! Her mother is 81 years old and now she beats the toffee bits with a hammer when she makes them for her friends so they don't break a crown. Prissy used them for every open house at the Ruby Begonia. They are quick, easy and the best tasting cookie you ever put in your mouth. Prissy used to do welcome bags for the visitors every Sunday at church. She had it down pat where she could make a whole batch of these cookies and bag them in one hour. Just make sure if you take them to someone or serve them to guests, have copies of the recipe to hand out! They're the best!*

**1 box butter yellow cake mix**
**⅔ c. oil**
**1 egg**
**1 (8 oz.) package of toffee bits**

Preheat oven to 350˚. Blend cake mix, oil and egg until it has a thick consistency, about 2 minutes. Fold in toffee bits.

Take about one T. of dough and roll into ball (This depends on what size cookie you want). Place on ungreased cookie sheet. Bake approximately 10 to 15 minutes. Keep a close watch. When they start to smell, they are just about done!

# White Chocolate
## Bread Pudding

*Mickey Orton, my cousin, and I love to cook. We love to hand sew. We love our families. These next recipes come from her kitchen in Sylacauga, Alabama. I know they are wonderful. Chocolate lovers will be in heaven! I love you dearly sweet sister/cousin!*

**1 lb. French bread**
**1 qt. heavy whipping cream**
**3 eggs**
**2 c. sugar**
**2 T. vanilla**
**2 (12 oz.) packages white chocolate chips**
**1 c. heavy whipping cream (for sauce)**

Tear bread into pieces and pour 1 quart of the heavy whipping cream over bread. Let stand for 15 minutes, stirring occasionally. Beat eggs, add sugar, vanilla and stir 1 package of white chocolate chips into bread mixture and mix together. Pour into greased 13 x 9 inch casserole dish and bake at 350˚ for 45 minutes to one hour or until brown on top.
For sauce: Melt one cup heavy cream and 1 package of white chocolate chips for about 1 minute in microwave. Stir until melted and smooth. Serve warm over bread.

# Mickey's Frozen Oreo Cookie Coffee Ice Cream Cake

**Crust:**
24 Oreo cookies, crushed
⅓ c. melted stick butter

**Filling:**
Remainder of stick of butter from crust (⅙ c.), melted
1 c. sugar
½ gallon coffee ice cream
3 squares unsweetened chocolate
½ tsp. vanilla
½ pt. whipping cream
¼ c. Tia Maria Liquer or Kahlua
¼ c. powdered sugar
1 jar of butterscotch sauce
Chopped pecans

To prepare crust, mix together 24 Oreo cookies, crushed and ⅓ cup melted butter. Pat mixture into 9 x 13 inch buttered Pyrex dish or baking pan and freeze. Layer softened coffee ice cream over cookie crust and refreeze. Prepare chocolate sauce in top of double boiler. Add remaining butter, 1 cup sugar to melted butter and 3 squares unsweetened chocolate. Cook over low heat for about 30 minutes. Stirring often. Do not boil. Remove from heat. Add ½ teaspoon vanilla and allow to come to room temperature before spreading over ice cream layer. Freeze. May use jar of chocolate hot fudge sauce if preferred. Prepare ½ pint whipping cream by adding ¼ cup Tia Maria Liqueur or Kahlua. Add ¼ cup powdered sugar. Whip all together until soft peaks form layer on top of frozen chocolate layer. Freeze. Spread top with 1 jar of butterscotch or caramel sauce and cover entire surface with chopped pecans. Cut in squares and serve immediately or cover with plastic wrap and store in freezer until ready to serve. May be necessary to dip knife in warm water to cut into squares if frozen.

# Phyllis' New Orleans Bread Pudding

*Bob always says, "Find one friend you want in the fox hole with you and that is a friend you can trust your life with." That's Phyllis Brooks for me! We've been through soooo much together. She's my girls' second mother, and my mother was her second mother. Every major event in life, we've been there for each other. A true friend loves at all times. Thanks, for always being there!*

1 loaf French bread, torn into chunks
1 qt. milk
2 c. sugar, or to taste
2 T. vanilla
3 eggs
1 c. peeled, diced apples
½ c. raisins
3-6 T. butter, melted

Soak bread in milk for about 30 minutes. Mix sugar, vanilla, eggs and apples. Combine with bread (I usually mix bread with potato masher so it won't be too chunky). Spread melted butter on bottom of 13x9 inch pan. Add bread mixture. To make pudding richer, I add melted butter to the bread. Bake at 350˚ for 30-35 minutes until bubbly and hot.

Sauce:
½ c. butter
1 c. sugar
1 tsp. vanilla
1 egg
Rum to taste, about 3 T. of rum flavoring

Cream butter and sugar. Add vanilla. Slowly stir in 1 egg. Add the rum. Heat and stir over low heat, about 5 minutes. Serve warm over individual pudding servings.

# Granny Hill's Chocolate Gravy

2 c. sugar
2 T. cocoa
1 tsp. salt
1 c. milk
1 tsp. vanilla flavoring
3 T. butter or margarine
2 T. flour

Combine sugar, salt, cocoa and flour. Add milk. Cook over medium heat until boiling. Let boil to a soft syrup effect. Do not overcook. It will harden after you remove from heat. Add vanilla and butter. Pour over hot buttered biscuits.

# Governor Riley's Favorite Oysters Rockefeller Casserole

*This will always bring a smile and lots of compliments.*

3 (10 oz.) packages frozen chopped spinach, thawed and drained
1 ⅔ c. green onions, chopped
1 c. celery, chopped
1 large garlic clove, crushed
1 tsp. thyme
1 ½ c. (3 sticks) butter, melted
1 ½ c. bread crumbs
1 T. Worcestershire sauce
1 tsp. anchovy paste
4 dz. small oysters
½ c. oyster liquor
¾ c. parsley, chopped
½ c. (2 oz.) grated Parmesan cheese
2 T. Pernod (anise-flavored liqueur)
½ tsp. salt
¼ tsp. black pepper
¼ tsp. cayenne pepper

Cook the spinach according to the package instructions. Drain. In a skillet, sauté the green onions, celery, garlic and thyme in butter for 5 minutes. Add the bread crumbs, Worcestershire sauce and anchovy paste. Cook for 5 minutes or until the bread crumbs are toasted, stirring constantly. Fold in the oysters, oyster liquor, parsley, cheese and liqueur. Cook for 3 minutes or until the edges of the oysters curl. Add the spinach, salt, black pepper and cayenne pepper and stir well. Spoon in a 3 quart casserole. Bake at 375° for 20 to 25 minutes. (Note: This dish may be cooked in ramekins and served as appetizers.)

# Penne Pasta with Lemon Butter Caper Sauce

*Our time serving this great state has been made even more meaningful because of the great people that have come into our lives to work with us. We are only as good as our staff and I appreciate so very much those who help me represent Alabama every day and love us on our best and worst days. This recipe comes from our newlywed, Leah Southern Dean, my executive assistant.*

3 boneless chicken breasts, grilled
1 ½ c. baby portabella mushrooms, sliced
2 ears of corn on the cob, chargrilled
16 oz. box of penne pasta, cooked
2-3 T. pine nuts
2 T. black sesame seeds
½ c. fresh parsley, chopped
½ c. fresh chives, chopped
2 large garlic cloves, minced
Salt and pepper
Sea Salt
Butter (for sautéing, use as needed)
Extra Virgin Olive Oil (for sautéing, use as needed)

Salt and pepper both sides of chicken (touch of sea salt). Grill. Cut into chunks after grilling and set aside. Grill two ears of corn. Cut off corn kernels after grilling. Set aside. Sauté mushrooms in olive oil. Add salt and pepper, garlic and slice of butter. Cook down, stirring occasionally on medium low heat. Prepare pasta (big pinch of salt, splash of olive oil in water) cook and drain. Set aside. Add chicken, corn, sesame seeds, pine nuts and pasta to sautéed ingredients. Simmer on low heat for 5 minutes. Stir occasionally. Remove from heat. Top dish with parsley and chives. Squeeze ½ lemon over dish. Pour Lemon Butter Caper Sauce on top. Toss and serve.

Lemon Butter Caper Sauce:
2 T. capers
2 lemons, freshly squeezed
½ c. Extra Virgin Olive Oil
1 stick butter, melted

Combine ingredients. Stir well over low heat. Reduce down.

Yield: 6 servings

# Southern Tomato Pie

*Debra Southern is a wonderful cook and a wonderful mother to my assistant Leah. We've had some fabulous days together from our first days in Montgomery, to Leah's wedding and all the days in between!*

1 regular 9 inch cooked pie crust
5 Roma tomatoes
½ tsp. dry basil
½ tsp. salt
1 c. mayonnaise
½ c. shredded Cheddar cheese
½ c. shredded mozzarella cheese

Cook the piecrust as directed and let cool.

Peel and slice tomatoes. Drain on paper towel. Place tomatoes in pie crust. Sprinkle tomatoes with salt and basil. Mix together mayonnaise and cheese. Pour mixture over tomatoes. Bake at 350˚ for 30 minutes.

# Nana's Apple Cake

*Hollon is new to our staff and a fellow lady of Clay County. This particular cake comes from Hollon's grandmother, Helen Bailey of Wadley, Alabama. Mrs. Bailey would make this cake as a sign that fall had arrived for her children when they were little and in school. Hollon's mother, Donna McKay, carried the tradition on to her children and made it each year when the seasons changed. The apples, dates and sugary glaze make this cake a delicious way to start the fall season.*

1 ½ c. Crisco oil
2 tsp. vanilla
2 c. sugar
3 c. plain flour
1 tsp. baking soda
3 c. chopped apples
1 tsp. salt
1 (8 oz) pkg. chopped dates
3 eggs
1 c. chopped pecans

Preheat oven to 350˚. In mixer, mix oil, sugar, eggs and vanilla. Sift together flour, soda and salt. Add to egg mixture. Beat with mixer until blended well. Add apples, dates, and pecans. Stir only enough to moisten. Pour in large tube pan (or two loaf pans) and bake 1 hour or until done at 350˚.

*This cake improves with age, but it is rarely afforded the opportunity.*

Glaze:
1 cup light brown sugar
1 stick butter
½ cup sweet milk

Cook for 3 minutes. Pour over hot cake (punch holes in cake using a knife or long skewer). Let cake remain in pan(s) for 2 hours.

# Mrs. Donna's Coconut Pound Cake

*Donna Bailey McKay became a dear friend to the Riley family a few years back when she became our Minda's fourth grade teacher. Well, here we are years later and our lives are connected again, as her beautiful daughter is my newest staff member and has done a wonderful job working on this cookbook. Thank you, Donna for this mouth watering coconut pound cake and for raising such a truly southern lady in Hollon.*

> 6 large eggs
> 1 c. butter flavored Crisco
> 1 stick margarine
> 3 c. sugar
> 1 tsp. almond extract
> 1 tsp. coconut extract
> 3 c. sifted cake flour
> 1 c. milk
> 2 c. packaged or fresh flaked coconut

Preheat the oven to 300°. Grease and flour a 10 inch tube pan. Separate the eggs. Set the whites aside and allow to come to room temperature. Beat the egg yolks with the Crisco and butter at high speed until well blended. Gradually add the sugar, beating until light and fluffy. Add the extracts and beat. At low speed, beat the flour (about one-quarter at a time) alternating with the milk (about ⅓ at a time). Begin and end with the flour. Add the coconut and beat on medium speed until well-blended.
In a clean bowl, beat the egg whites until stiff peaks form. Gently fold the whites into the batter. Pour into the prepared pan. Bake for 2 hours. Cool the cake in the pan on a wire rack for 15 minutes. Remove from the pan and finish cooling on a rack.

# Pimento Cheese Salad

*This recipe is from Jan Dismuke, a cousin of our Governor and a special part of our family. Her mother, Winnell Ingram Riley, was very dear to my heart and I was blessed to have experienced many of the wonderful dishes she prepared. Jan tells me this recipe is somewhat different from a lot of salads I have tried. I hope everyone will enjoy it as much as Jan's family has over the years. Jan, you are always there for me in my happiest hours and in my grief. I love you, dear one.*

> 4 oz. jar of pimento
> 6 oz. sharp Cheddar cheese, grated
> ½ to ¾ c. mayonnaise
> 1 ½ tsp. sugar
> 2 small boxes of lemon Jell-O or 1 large box
> 1 can (12 oz.) unsweetened crushed pineapple drained (save liquid for Jell-O)
> 8 oz. cream cheese (room temp.)
> ⅓ c. finely chopped celery
> ½ c. chopped pecans or walnuts
> 1 pt. heavy whipping cream
> ¾ c. pimento cheese

Mix Jell-O with 2 c. boiling water and 1 c. of pineapple juice. Let partially set. Mix cream cheese, pineapple and pimento cheese together until blended. Add to partially set Jell-O and mix together. Stir in celery and nuts. Whip cream with 1 ½ tsp. sugar. Fold into Jell-O mixture. Let congeal overnight.

# Happy Days
## and Holidays

*Notes*

# Happy Days and Holidays

I've received so many wonderful cookbooks. I know Alabama has some of the best cooks in the world simply by reading and cooking out of these great books.

Here are a few of the great dishes I've enjoyed cooking while I've been First Lady of Alabama and some new recipes I hope to enjoy cooking and adding to my holiday joy.

## Creamy Shrimp Pastry Shells

*I discovered this recipe one Christmas. We all agree this is a tradition at the Riley House.*

1 ½ lbs. medium-size fresh shrimp
⅔ c. dry white wine
2 T. fresh parsley, chopped
½ tsp. salt
½ c. chopped onion
3 T. butter
3 T. all-purpose flour
1 c. milk
1 c. shredded Swiss cheese
2 tsp. lemon juice
½ tsp. pepper
2 pkg. frozen phyllo pastry shells, baked

Combine wine and next three ingredients in a saucepan. Bring to a low boil. Chop shrimp into small pieces. Add shrimp to wine mixture and cook three to five minutes. Drain and reserve ¼ c. liquid. Melt butter in a large saucepan over low heat. Add flour, stirring until smooth. Cook one minute, stirring constantly. Slowly add milk. Cook over medium heat, stirring until mixture is thickened and bubbly. Add Swiss cheese, stirring until cheese melts. Gradually stir in ½ c. wine, lemon juice, and pepper. Spoon mixture into pastry shells. Bake for five minutes at 250° or until pastry shells are browned.

## Wassail

*Christmas wouldn't be Christmas without Wassail at the Riley House or the Governor's Mansion! People will see me in the grocery store and ask about my wassail recipe. It'll bring Christmas cheer! Now we make wassail by the gallons at the mansion. It just has a special warm way of saying, "Welcome" and "Merry Christmas!"*

1 gal. apple juice or cider
1 qt. orange juice
1 c. lemon juice
1 qt. pineapple juice
24 whole cloves
4 sticks cinnamon
1 c. sugar

Combine all ingredients and simmer for 10 minutes. Remove cinnamon and cloves after 30 minutes. Do not boil. Serve warm in punch cups or Christmas mugs.

*Tip: Wassail freezes great. Pour wassail into ice trays (remember those?) and freeze. Place one cube, heat and you have one cup at a time for wassail time.*

# Chicken Asparagus Casserole

*There is never enough left of this casserole to have leftovers. This has been in my file for more than 40 years. It came to me by Mary Frances Pruet of Ashland, Alabama, in 1965. I believe I've cooked this for every Christmas holiday since then. Everyone loves it and it's a real tradition at the Riley holiday table.*

4 chicken breasts, with bones
1 small box white rice
1 large can asparagus, drained
(<u>reserve juice</u>)
1 ½ c. Cheddar cheese
1 c. almonds, slivered
½ stick butter, melted

Boil chicken until tender. I add a few dashes of garlic salt and a pat of butter in the water. Drain after cooking. When cooled, pull meat from bones. Cook rice according to directions. Place rice in large oblong casserole. Place drained asparagus spears on top of rice bed along with chicken pieces. Make a medium white sauce, but instead of using only milk, replace half the milk with the juice from asparagus. Pour sauce over rice, chicken and asparagus. Top with cheese and almonds. Pour melted butter over almonds and bake 40 minutes at 350˚ or until bubbles and almonds are golden brown.

**Basic White Sauce:**
4 T. butter
4 T. flour
½ tsp. salt
dash pepper
2 c. milk or half & half

*Tip: It will take 2 recipes of white sauce. Using half & half instead of milk will get a richer white sauce.*

# Miss Anne Gran's Pralines

*I'll miss lots of things when we leave Montgomery, but I'll truly miss my pop-in visits at Richardson's Drugstore. Maybe it reminds me of my Daddy's drugstore and maybe I love their gifts, but I mostly love the stationery and the people. Nothing takes the place of a family owned business! Miss Anne has helped me many times with notes and encouragement. And she helped me get the Governor well from the flu! From behind her computer and printer, she's a pretty good doctor!*

5 c. sugar
1 14 oz. can condensed milk
1 c. regular milk
5 c. pecans
1 T. salt
1 stick butter
1 T. vanilla

Combine sugar and milks in a large heavy saucepan and let mixture come to a boil. Add pecans and boil 20 minutes stirring constantly. Remove from heat and add salt, butter and vanilla. Beat. Test by dropping a small amount in a ½ c. cold water. When it is forming a hard ball, spoon mixture on waxed paper and let cool. This makes six dozen.

# Mother's Always Best Pecan Pie

*As a child, I remember Mama baking this pie. Now I make sure I have at least two at Thanksgiving!*

3 eggs, slightly beaten
1 c. Karo syrup (dark)
⅛ tsp. salt
1 c. sugar
1 c. pecans
1 tsp. vanilla
¼ c. melted butter

Beat eggs slightly. Add sugar and beat again. Add syrup, melted butter and pecans. Mix well. Pour into pie shell. Bake 10 minutes at 400˚. Reduce heat to 325˚. Bake until custard is firm.

*Tip: Pecan pies do burn quickly. Adjust oven temperature to what works well with your oven.*

# Foolproof Flaky Pastry

1 c. sifted all-purpose flour
½ tsp. salt
½ T. vinegar
3 T. shortening

Sift together the measured flour and salt. Cut in shortening with 2 knives or a pastry blender until particles in mixture are the size of small peas. Sprinkle water and vinegar over the mixture. Toss with a fork until particles stick together. Form pastry into a small ball. Wrap dough in waxed paper and chill. Lightly sprinkle flour on board and rolling pin. Roll the pastry into a circle one inch larger than pie plate. Place in pie pan and crimp edges or shape with tines of fork. Prick crust on bottom and sides before baking. Bake the pie shell in a 450˚ oven for about 12 minutes or until brown. Cool and fill.

# My Daddy's Favorite Fudge

*Daddy loved chocolate! Chocolate candy, chocolate ice cream and chocolate sauce. He could eat a pound of it and never gain a pound! I made him a box of fudge for Christmas every year and put it under the tree.*

½ c. cocoa - more if you like a dark chocolate, less if you want a milk chocolate
3 c. sugar
1 ½ c. half & half or whole milk
1 pinch salt to ⅛ tsp.
½ stick butter
1 tsp. vanilla
1 c. pecans, chopped

Mix cocoa, sugar and salt. Stir in half & half. When sugar mixture dissolves, place on heat. Bring to a full rolling boil. Reduce heat, a slow boil is needed. Cook about 20 minutes, or until it gets thick and loses its glossy shine. Add pecans, butter and vanilla and cook a little longer. Remove from heat. Beat well with a wooden spoon until it gets dull in shine. Pour onto a large cookie sheet that has been buttered. Let cool. Cut into squares.

*Tip: I use a pizza cutter to cut the warm candy into squares.*

## Vidalia Onion Dip

*This is soooo good, but be sure to always use Hellman's mayo. I love to have this waiting for family, friends or guests when they arrive for the holidays or any time of year.*

2 c. Vidalia onions, chopped
2 c. sharp Cheddar cheese, grated
1 c. Hellman's mayonnaise (must use Hellman's)

Mix and bake at 350° for 30 to 40 minutes until center is heated well. Serve with bagel chips.

## Miss Patsy's Favorite No-fail Peanut Brittle

*You'll need to plan on more than one recipe of this peanut brittle for Christmas Eve.*

1 c. light corn syrup
2 T. margarine
1 c. sugar
¼ c. water
1 ½ c. salted peanuts
1 tsp. baking soda

A candy thermometer is a must for this recipe. In heavy sauce pot, combine corn syrup, margarine, sugar and water. Bring to a boil over medium heat. When mixture starts to boil do not stir. Insert candy thermometer and cook until temperature reaches 280°. Add peanuts, gradually stirring. Cook until temperature reaches 300°. Remove immediately from heat. Add baking soda and beat well. Pour onto a well-greased cookie sheet with sides. Ready to eat in about 5 minutes. Crack and serve.

## Cranberry Apple Salad

*With a hint of orange and sparkling red, this cranberry-apple mold is sure to brighten your Christmas buffet. I can remember Mama grinding whole fresh cranberries for this Christmas salad. Mama used individual molds garnished with a spoonful of mayo and sprinkled with chopped nuts and a mint leaf.*

1 (3 oz.) package raspberry-flavored gelatin
¾ c. boiling water
1 (8 oz.) can crushed pineapple, drained
1 (16 oz.) can whole-berry cranberry sauce
1 Red Delicious apple, unpeeled and coarsely chopped
1 T. chopped orange meat
1 c. pecans
⅛ tsp. salt
⅛ tsp. ground cinnamon
Dash of ground cloves
Lettuce leaves
Garnishes: fresh cranberries and orange rind strips

Dissolve raspberry flavored gelatin in boiling water and let cool. Stir in next 7 ingredients and spoon into a lightly oiled 4 cup mold. Cover and chill until firm. Unmold on lettuce leaves. Garnish if desired.

Yield: 8 servings

# Holly and Berry Candy

*I've been making this since Rob was in the 3rd grade. One of the room mothers brought these to school and it's been a Riley treat ever since!*

1 package large marshmallows
1 stick butter
1 tsp. vanilla
Green food coloring - enough to get a deep Christmas green
Red hots
4 to 6 c. corn flakes

Melt butter on low heat. Add marshmallows, vanilla and food coloring. Melt completely. Add enough flakes to be coated well with marshmallow mixture. Spoon mixture onto buttered cookie sheet or waxed paper. Shape like holly leaves. Place three or four red hots to look like berries. Let cool before removing from cookie sheet.

# Thanksgiving Pumpkin Pie

*Bob loves pumpkin pie. So for many years, Minda always baked her Daddy a pumpkin pie on Thanksgiving Eve for our dinner the next night. Now that she has her own family and every other year she has her own family dinner, I have to bake his pie. I miss Minda on these years, not just because she does a great job on the pie, but I miss our time in the kitchen together*

1 (15 oz.) pkg. Pillsbury® All Ready Pie Crusts
1 tsp. flour
2 eggs, slightly beaten
1 (16 oz.) can Libby's Solid Pack Pumpkin
¾ c. sugar
½ tsp. salt
1 tsp. ground cinnamon
½ tsp. ground ginger
¼ tsp. ground cloves
1 (12 oz.) can Carnation Evaporated Milk

Heat oven to 425°. Prepare one pie crust according to package directions. Refrigerate remaining pie crust for later use. Flute edge to stand ½ inch above rim. Mix filling ingredients in order given. Pour into pie crust lined pan. Bake at 425° for 15 minutes. Reduce heat to 350° and continue baking for 35 to 45 minutes or until knife inserted near center of pie comes out clean. If necessary, cover edge of crust with a strip of aluminum foil to prevent excessive browning. Cool completely. Garnish, if desired, with whipped topping.

# Christmas Cheese Ball

*A cheese ball is a nice treat to have waiting for family and friends when they walk through the door and hear, "Merry Christmas!"*

2 (8 oz.) packages cream cheese, softened
4 c. shredded Cheddar cheese
½ c. sour cream
1 package dry Italian salad dressing mix
1 c. chopped pecans
1 onion, chopped
½ c. dry parsley
Pecan halves and green olives for garnish

Mix all ingredients except chopped nuts and dry parsley. Mix well. Shape into 2 small or 1 large ball. Coat with chopped nuts and dry parsley. Chill 8 hours. Garnish with pecan halves and green olives. Serve with crackers.

# Baked Spiced Fruit

*I've had this recipe for about 35 years. It's one I sometimes forget for a year or two. Then I pull it out of my cooking file box. It's wonderful with baked ham or turkey.*

1 (16 oz.) fruit cocktail
1 (17 oz.) can apricot halves
1 (16 oz.) can peach halves
1 (16 oz.) can pear halves
1 (15 ¼ oz.) can pineapple chunks
1 c. orange juice
½ c. firmly packed brown sugar
1 T. lemon juice
1 jar red cherries
1 banana, sliced
4 whole cloves
½ c. red cooking wine
1 c. chopped pecans
½ stick butter, cut up
1 can apple sauce

Drain fruit, reserving syrup for other uses. Cut apricot, peach and pear halves in half. Combine fruit in a large oblong baking dish. Combine orange juice and remaining ingredients in a saucepan. Bring to a boil, reduce heat and simmer two minutes. Pour over fruit. Pour wine and top with small amount of brown sugar and apple sauce. Nuts go on last with butter. Bake at 350° for 30 minutes. Serve hot.

# Miss Peggy's Kisses

*Every year at Christmas time, Miss Peggy from Ashland always baked my favorite confections. One that Bob loves is "Kisses!" I do not have her recipe, but I have found this one and I believe this is very close to her wonderful traditional recipe. Kisses under the mistletoe and kisses I dish out… for all to enjoy! It will be a very Merry Christmas and a Happy New Year!*

3 egg whites
½ tsp. creme of tartar
1 c. brown sugar
1 c. pecans, finely chopped

Beat egg whites until stiff. Add creme of tartar while beating. Slowly beat in sugar, beat well. Fold in nuts. Spoon onto greased cookie sheet and bake at 200° for 1 ½ to 2 hours.

# Red Velvet Holiday Punch

*Bob and I share the same opinion when it comes to picking our favorite high school teacher. It would be Mrs. Lila Jordan. She will always be a sweet memory. She gave me this recipe when I was a young bride. I've used it for every party I have hosted the past 44 years!*

1 (3 oz.) pkg. strawberry, or orange, or lime Jell-O
1 c. sugar
2 c. boiling water
4 c. cold water
2 (6 oz.) frozen lemonade, mixed according to directions
1 large can pineapple juice
1 large bottle ginger ale, cold

Mix Jell-O and sugar. Add hot water. Stir until dissolved. Add cold water and lemonade. Stir. Add pineapple juice and stir well. Freeze in plastic jug or container until it is a hard slush. Pour into punch bowl. Add cold ginger ale. This is a great holiday, party or wedding punch!

# Holiday Ice Ring

The day before serving your punch, prepare a pretty ice ring by boiling about 7 c. of water for 1 minute. Let cool at room temperature. (This eliminates cloudiness in the ice ring that water straight from the tap can cause.) Pour 3 c. of the water into a 6-cup ring mold and freeze. Set remaining water aside.

Cut a thin slice from the bottom of a lemon, lime or orange using a sharp paring knife. Discard the bottom. Beginning at the top, peel a continuous strip ½ to ¾ inch wide. Starting with the first por-

tion cut and shape the strip like a rose. Coil tightly at first to form the center, gradually coiling more loosely to form the outer petals. Repeat this process for each citrus rose.

Slice lemons, limes or oranges and cut slices in half. Arrange citrus roses, sliced citrus halves and mint leaves on top of ice in the ring. Slowly fill the mold to top with remaining water. Freeze. To unmold, let the mold sit at room temperature 5 minutes or until loosened. Carefully float ice ring in punch. This ring shows up better if punch isn't a slush.

# New Year's Eve Chicken Salad Pie

*I love to get a big fire going, get into my kitchen in Ashland and start cooking for New Year's Eve. We enjoy this with cranberry salad and hot rolls. As we bring in the New Year, a hint of sadness always overcomes me. However, life goes on and soon we are well into a new untouched year, with new goals and new dreams, and lately new grandbabies!*

3 c. chicken, cooked
1 c. diced celery
½ c. slivered almonds, toasted
½ tsp. salt
1 T. grated onion
2 T. fresh lemon juice
1 ½ c. mayonnaise
1 can water chestnuts, chopped
1 c. shredded cheese
1 (8 inch) pie shell

Mix all ingredients. Pour in pie shell. Bake 30 minutes at 375˚. Sprinkle cheese on top.

## Party Anytime
## Bit-of-Brie Appetizer

¾ c. finely chopped pecans
¼ c. Kahlua or other coffee
flavored liqueur
3 T. brown sugar
1 (14 oz.) mini Brie

Spread pecans in a 9 inch pie plate and
microwave at high 4 to 6 minutes, stirring every 2 minutes until toasted. Add
Kahlua and sugar. Stir well.
Remove rind from top of Brie and discard. Place Brie on a microwave safe
serving plate. Spoon pecan mixture
over top of Brie. Microwave, uncovered,
on high 1 to 2 minutes or until Brie
softens to desired consistency. Give
dish a half-turn after 1 minute. Serve
with Melba toast or crackers.

Yield: 12 servings

## Pineapple Upside Down Cake

3 T. butter or margarine
½ c. firmly packed brown sugar
1 (8 oz.) can sliced pineapple,
drained
12 maraschino cherries
⅔ c. chopped pecans
¼ c. shortening
1 c. sugar
2 eggs
1 ½ c. all-purpose flour
2 tsp. baking powder
½ tsp. salt
½ c. milk
1 tsp. vanilla extract

Melt butter in a 10 inch cast-iron skillet. Spread brown sugar evenly over
butter. Arrange pineapple and cherries
on sugar. Top with pecans.
Combine shortening and sugar. Beat
well at medium speed of an electric
mixer. Add eggs, one at a time. Beat
well after each addition.
Combine flour, baking powder and salt.
Add to creamed mixture alternately
with milk, beginning and ending with
flour mixture. Stir in vanilla. Spoon batter evenly over pineapple slices. Bake
at 350˚ for 45-50 minutes or until cake
tests done. Cool cake 5 minutes and
invert onto plate.

Yield: One 10 inch cake

## Happy Birthday Spoon Rolls

1 package dry yeast
2 c. warm water (105˚-115˚)
½ c. butter or margarine, melted
4 c. self-rising flour
1 egg, slightly beaten
¼ c. sugar

Dissolve yeast in warm water and let
stand 5 minutes. Combine yeast mixture,
butter and flour in a large bowl, mixing
well. Stir in egg and sugar. (Mixture will
be a very soft batter.) Cover and refrigerate batter overnight. Spoon batter into
greased muffin pans, filling two-thirds full.
Bake at 350˚ for 25 minutes.

Yield: 16 rolls

Note: Batter may be stored and covered in refrigerator up to 4 days.

# Welcome Home
# Stuffed Chicken Breasts

*This is a great way to say, "Welcome Home."*

2 large chicken breast halves
(about ⅔ lb.), skinned and boned
¼ c. chopped onion
3 T. chopped green pepper
1 small clove garlic, minced
2 T. butter or margarine, melted
⅔ c. herb-seasoned stuffing mix
⅓ c. water
⅛ tsp. salt
⅛ tsp. pepper
2 T. butter or margarine, melted
½ c. cream of chicken soup,
undiluted
2 T. dry white wine
1 T. herb-seasoned stuffing mix
Garnish: chopped parsley

Place each piece of chicken between 2
sheets of wax paper. Flatten to ¼ inch
thickness using a meat mallet or rolling
pin. Set aside.

Sauté onion, green pepper and garlic in
2 T. butter. Stir in ⅔ c. stuffing mix and
next 3 ingredients.

Spread stuffing mixture evenly on each
chicken breast, leaving a ½ inch margin
on all sides. Fold short ends of chicken
over stuffing. Roll up, beginning with one
unfolded side. Secure with wooden picks.
Brown chicken in 2 T. butter. Place in
a 9 inch pie plate. Combine soup and
wine. Pour over chicken. Sprinkle with
1 T. herb seasoned stuffing mix. Cover
with aluminum foil and bake at 325°
for 50 minutes or until done. Garnish,
if desired.

Yield: 2 servings

# Holiday Orange Balls

*These can turn any table into a holiday
table.*

1 (7 ½ oz.) box vanilla wafers
¾ c. confectioners' sugar
1 (3 ½ oz.) can coconut
½ c. frozen orange juice concentrate
Confectioners' sugar for coating

Crush vanilla wafers. Mix all ingredients and shape into marble size balls.
Roll balls in confectioners' sugar. Chill
overnight. Next morning, put into paper
bag and shake in confectioners' sugar
to thoroughly coat.

Yield: 4 dozen

# Fruit and Nut Balls

*These are a very healthy treat!*

½ c. shelled walnuts
½ c. shelled almonds
½ c. seeded raisins
1 c. pecans
8 pitted dates
3 dried figs
Confectioner's sugar

Chop or grind nuts and fruit. Sprinkle
a little confectioners' sugar on a
breadboard and knead the mixture until
it's thoroughly blended. Shape into
balls. Roll in chopped nuts and sugar if
desired.

# Good Morning and Merry Christmas Speedy Orange Rolls

1 package dry yeast
½ c. warm water (105° - 115°)
2 to 2 ¼ c. all-purpose flour, divided
2 T. butter or margarine, softened
1 T. sugar
1 tsp. salt
1 egg, beaten
Orange Filling

Dissolve yeast in warm water in a large mixing bowl. Let stand 5 minutes. Add 1 c. flour and next 4 ingredients. Beat at medium speed of an electric mixer until smooth. Stir in remaining flour to make a soft dough.

Turn dough out onto a lightly floured surface. Knead until smooth (about 2 minutes). Cover and let stand 15 minutes. Roll dough into a 14 x 7 inch rectangle. Spread with half of orange filling, leaving a 1 inch margin on long sides. Roll dough jellyroll fashion, starting at long side. Pinch seam to seal (do not seal ends). Cut into 12 equal slices. Place slices, cut side down, in greased muffin pans. Cover and let rise in a warm place (85°), free from drafts for 30 minutes. Bake at 400° for 16 to 18 minutes. Spread remaining orange filling over tops of rolls.

Yield: 12 rolls

Orange Filling:
1 ½ c. sifted powdered sugar
½ T. grated orange rind
3 T. butter or margarine, melted
2 T. orange juice

Combine all ingredients, stirring well.

Yield: about ½ cup

# Early or Late New Year's Breakfast Orange-Nut Bread

2 ¼ c. sifted flour, plain
2 ¼ tsp. baking powder
¼ tsp. soda
¾ tsp. salt
¾ c. sugar
¾ c. chopped nuts
2 T. melted shortening
1 beaten egg
¾ c. orange juice
1 T. orange peel, grated

Sift dry ingredients into a large mixing bowl. Add nuts, melted shortening, egg, orange juice and grated peel. Shortening should be at room temperature so it won't separate from other ingredients. Stir until mixture is dampened but not smooth. Pour into an 8 ½ x 4 ½ inch loaf pan. Bake at 350° for 55 minutes.

# French Fried Peanuts
*Wow! I can't wait to try these with my grandkids.*

Heat deep fryer to 375° and place peanuts in hot oil for 4 minutes. Take peanuts out. Drain on paper towel. Place on large platter and sprinkle with salt.

# Tea Cakes or Christmas Cookies

*This is my Christmas cookie recipe I've used for 43 years. We have such sweet memories of family time decorating our cookies on Christmas Eve. This is such a wonderful cookie base for Valentine's Day, Easter or any holiday cutout cookie. I keep these times close to my heart, and I hope all my children and grandchildren will remember our times as fondly as I do.*

⅔ c. oleo
1 ¼ c. sugar
2 eggs
3 c. plain flour
2 tsp. baking powder
1 ½ tsp. salt
1 tsp. vanilla

Cream butter and sugar. Add eggs one at a time. Add dry ingredients and vanilla. Chill for one hour. Roll out thin on floured cloth. Cut out and bake until brown. Bake at 325˚. Place cookies on well greased cookie sheet.

*Tip: If your cookie dough is too stiff, add a little water. Blend. Then chill.*

# Party Time Sweet-n-Sour Meatballs

*These are quick to make and go a long way for drop-in company or Christmas Eve Buffet.*

Meatballs:
1 c. quick-cooking oatmeal
⅓ c. milk
1 lb. ground beef
½ tsp. onion powder
1 tsp. garlic salt
1 T. soy sauce
½ tsp. hot sauce
1 small can water chestnuts

Soak oatmeal in milk. Squeeze out excess liquid. Add oatmeal to ground beef. Add seasonings. Drain water chestnuts and mince fine. Add to ground beef and mix thoroughly. Shape into small balls (bite size). Brown in 350˚ oven for 20 minutes. Do not turn.

Sweet-n-Sour Sauce:
1 (13 ½ oz.) can pineapple chunks
2 T. cornstarch
½ c. vinegar
½ c. brown sugar
2 T. soy sauce
2 T. lemon juice
1 c. coarsely chopped green pepper
1 T. chopped pimento (optional)

Drain pineapple chunks. Save syrup. Measure pineapple syrup and add enough water to make 1 cup. Blend together pineapple liquid and cornstarch until smooth. Stir in next four ingredients. Cook until thickened and clear. Add pineapple, green pepper and pimento. Mix well. Cover and simmer over low heat 15 minutes. Add meatballs and serve warm with wooden picks.

Yield: 20 meatballs

# Potato Chip Cookies

*I have eaten these at a tea. They're great! Thank you Rachel Meads of Birmingham, Alabama. These will have your guests asking, "What is this wonderful little cookie?"*

2 c. margarine
1 c. sugar
2 tsp. vanilla
3 c. plain flour
1 ½ c. crushed chips

Beat margarine and sugar until fluffy. Gradually add flour and vanilla to mixture. Add chips last and beat together. Drop by teaspoon on greased cookie sheet and bake on 350° for 10 to 12 minutes. Sprinkle with powdered sugar.

# Chicken Cheese Spread

*This is so quick and easy! Our younger cooks will love to prepare this for the family.*

1 large can premium chunk chicken, drained
8 oz. shredded Cheddar cheese
8 oz. cream cheese, softened
3 T. mayonnaise
½ package dry Ranch dip mix

Chop chicken and combine with all other ingredients. Refrigerate at least 2 hours. Serve with crackers.

# Governor's Pepper Steak

3 lbs. round steak (cubed)
1 c. celery
¾ c. salad oil

3 onions
3 cloves garlic
2 c. mushrooms
2 peppers (green)
2 T. soy sauce
6 tomatoes
La Choy noodles or rice
Steak sauce (mushroom steak sauce)

Marinate meat, garlic and salad oil for 1 hour. Brown meat. Add onion, pepper and celery. Cook on high temperature a short time. Add mushrooms and juice and tomatoes. Cook until tender. Add 2 cans mushroom steak sauce. Thicken with cornstarch. Serve over noodles or rice.

# Creamy Raspberry Vinaigrette

*Valentine's Day is another holiday I love. This will be a wonderful dressing for a romantic dinner for two.*

10 oz. package frozen raspberries, thawed
⅓ c. sugar
⅓ c. raspberry vinegar
¾ c. vegetable oil
½ c. light cream

Press raspberries through a fine sieve to puree. Set aside. In blender, combine sugar and vinegar until smooth. With blender off, slowly add oil and then slowly add cream. Add raspberry puree. Mix until smooth. Refrigerate until ready to serve.

# Heavenly Sunshine Lemon Cheese Cake

*This will bring sunshine to any day.*

**1 Duncan Hines White Cake Mix**

Mix according to directions. Grease and flour three 8 or 9 inch cake pans. Divide dough into the pans equally. Bake at 350˚ in pre-heated oven for 20 to 25 minutes. Cool completely. Spread with lemon cheese frosting.

> **Lemon Cheese Icing:**
> 1 ½ c. sugar
> 5 egg yolks (beaten)
> 1 whole egg
> Juice of 3 large lemons
> Grated rind of 1 lemon
> 1 stick of butter

Mix all together and cook in double boiler until very thick. Cool completely and spread between layers and on top of cake.

# Baked Shrimp

*This will become a favorite gulf, bay or land, holiday or any day recipe.*

> ¼ c. butter
> 1 (8 oz.) bottle commercial Italian dressing
> Juice of 2 lemons
> ¼ tsp. freshly ground pepper
> 3 lb. large shrimp, peeled with tails intact

Melt butter in a 13 x 9 inch baking dish. Add dressing, lemon juice and pepper. Add shrimp to sauce, mixing well. Bake at 325˚ for 25-30 minutes, stirring several times.

Yield: 6-8 servings

# Lemony Chicken

*This chicken recipe has a very different flavor. I think you'll enjoy the zest.*

> 1 qt. buttermilk
> 1 T. lemon zest (from 1 lemon)
> 4 boneless skinless chicken breasts, tenders removed, cut in strips
> 2 c. all-purpose flour
> 1 c. cornstarch
> Vegetable oil, for frying
>
> For Sauce:
> 1 (11 oz.) jar lemon curd
> ¼ c. chicken broth
> ¼ tsp. ground ginger
> ½ tsp. soy sauce

Add enough oil to cover the bottom of a large frying pan by ¼ to ½ inch depth. Heat oil to 365˚. Meanwhile, whisk buttermilk and lemon zest together in a medium bowl. Add chicken and set aside. Sift together flour and cornstarch into a shallow dish. Remove chicken from buttermilk mixture and dredge in flour mixture. Fry chicken strips until golden brown, about 4 to 5 minutes. Carefully flip chicken and continue cooking another 3 to 4 minutes. Drain on paper towels.

While chicken is frying, make the sauce. In a small saucepan, over low heat, melt lemon curd, stirring constantly. Add remaining ingredients and heat through. Drizzle sauce over chicken and serve.

# Apple Rice Pilaf with Toasted Almonds

*This is a side dish for any meal that will give your plate a new flair.*

1 T. butter
¼ onion, finely chopped
¼ Golden Delicious apple, finely chopped
2 c. apple juice
2 c. enriched long grain instant rice
¼ c. slivered almonds, toasted

In a medium saucepan, melt butter and sauté onion and apples over medium heat until soft. Add apple juice. Increase heat to high and bring to a boil. Stir in rice. Cover and remove from heat. Let stand for 5 minutes. Remove cover and stir in toasted almonds. Serve.

# First Lady's Favorite Smoked Oyster Dip

8 oz. cream cheese, softened
2 T. mayonnaise
1 tsp. lemon juice
¼ tsp. garlic salt
2 to 3 drops hot sauce
8 oz. can smoked oysters, drained
½ c. olives, chopped

In small mixing bowl, combine cream cheese, mayonnaise, lemon juice, garlic salt, hot sauce and mix until well blended. Chop drained oysters and fold into cheese mixture. Stir in chopped olives. Serve with your choice of crackers. Will keep refrigerated up to 3 days.

# Easy Mushroom Rice

*This is a great new side dish – Hope you enjoy.*

1 ½ c. uncooked long grain rice
1 (10 ¾ oz.) can cream of mushroom soup, undiluted
1 (2 oz.) jar diced pimento, drained
1 egg, slightly beaten
¼ tsp. pepper
½ c. slivered almonds, chopped
1 c. (4 oz) shredded sharp Cheddar cheese, divided

Cook rice according to package directions, omitting salt. Combine all ingredients except ¼ c. cheese. Mix well. Spoon mixture into a lightly greased 1 ½ quart casserole. Bake at 350˚ for 30 minutes. Sprinkle with remaining ¼ c. cheese and bake additional 10 minutes.

Yield: 6-8 servings

# GiGi's Party Mix

*As a little girl, I loved eating this healthy snack at Mama Mary Williams' house in Auburn, Alabama. She kept it in large glass jars in her kitchen. I love to keep party mix year round for my sweet grandbabies. It's quick to fix and great to keep on hand for hungry little visitors with big appetites.*

1 large box Nabisco rice squares
1 large box Nabisco wheat squares
1 large box Nabisco corn squares
1 Box Cheese Nips
2 Cans of mixed nuts
1 Box Cheerios
1 Box (or package) stick pretzels
1 Stick butter
1 cup Worcestershire sauce
3 T. Garlic Salt

Bake for 1 hour and serve.

*Tip: It's fun to add other oats and nuts to change it up a little.*

# The Best Ever Asparagus Tart

*These were served at a luncheon I attended. I almost got brave enough to ask for seconds! Wonderful!*

1 (9 inch) refrigerator pie pastry
1 lb. asparagus spears
2 thick slices hickory-smoked bacon
1 T. butter
¼ c. sweet onion, chopped
¼ c. red bell pepper, chopped
4 oz. cream cheese, softened
½ c. mayonnaise
½ c. half & half
2 T. all-purpose flour
2 eggs
2 c. (8 oz.) shredded Swiss cheese
1 c. (4 oz.) grated Parmesan cheese

Preheat the oven to 350˚. Fit the pie pastry into a lightly greased tart pan and bake for 5 to 7 minutes. Let stand until cool. Maintain the oven temperature.

Snap off the thick woody ends of the asparagus spears and discard. Cut the spears into 3 inch pieces. Bring 1 inch of water to a boil in a saucepan and place the asparagus in a steamer basket over the boiling water. Steam covered for 4 to 6 minutes or until tender-crisp and drain.

Cook the bacon in a skillet over medium high heat until crisp. Remove the bacon to a paper towel to drain, reserving the pan drippings. Cool the bacon and crumble. Melt the butter with the reserved pan drippings and add the onion and bell pepper. Sauté until tender.

Combine the cream cheese, mayonnaise, half and half, flour and eggs in a mixing bowl and beat until blended. Stir in the bacon, onion mixture and Swiss cheese. Arrange the asparagus in the baked shell and pour the cream cheese mixture over the top. Sprinkle with the Parmesan cheese and bake for 30 to 35 minutes or until a knife inserted near the center comes out clean.

Yield: 6–8 servings

# Aunt Sue's Sand Tarts

*Things are but poor substitutes for giving. The only true gift is a portion of yourself. I can't say I know anyone that will give of themselves anymore than Sue Riley. I read this Bible verse not long ago and it reminded me of my sister-in-law, Sue. "God has given each of us some special abilities. Be sure to use them to help each other, passing on to others God's many blessings." 1 Peter 4:10. She has many abilities and she uses them to help others.*

> 2 sticks butter
> 5 T. powdered sugar
> 1 ½ c. pecans, chopped
> 2 c. all-purpose flour
> 2 tsp. vanilla flavoring

Mix together and roll into one inch balls. Place on ungreased pan. Bake at 350° for approximately 30 minutes. Let cool slightly. Roll in sifted powdered sugar.

# Sugared Pansies

> 1 large egg white
> 1 T. water
> 20 to 30 pansies or other edible flowers, plus leaves if desired
> 1 c. superfine sugar

Whisk egg white with water. Place flowers on a wire rack. Using a small brush, barely moisten top and bottom of each petal with egg wash. Using tongs to hold flower by stem, sift superfine sugar over entire flower, turning to coat. Let dry on rack. Repeat with remaining flowers, leaving about 1/4 of them unsugared. (Sugared flowers are best the day you make them but can be stored in an airtight container for up to 3 days.) Just before serving, arrange sugared and unsugared flowers over the top of the cake.

# Recipes from
# First Families
# Across the United States

*Notes*

# Recipes from First Families Across the United States

## Alabama:
### Governor Bob Riley and First Lady Patsy Riley

*Alabama was the first state to declare Christmas a legal holiday in 1836. Alabama does not have an official nickname, but is commonly called "The Heart of Dixie."*

## Red Snapper with Butter and Shallot Sauce
*Very Elegant!*

**Crème Fraîche:**
½ c. heavy cream
½ c. sour cream

**Sauce:**
⅓ c. raspberry vinegar (see Note)
2 T. finely minced shallots
1 c. (2 sticks) chilled unsalted butter, cut into small pieces
1 T. crème fraîche

**Red Snapper:**
2 (¾ lb.) red snapper fillets
⅓ c. fish stock
⅓ c. dry white wine or vermouth
Salt and ground pepper (to taste)
3 c. finely shredded fresh spinach

For the crème fraîche: Whisk together the heavy cream and sour cream. Cover loosely with plastic wrap and let stand in a reasonably warm spot overnight or until thickened. Cover and refrigerate for 4 hours or until quite thick.

Preheat the oven to 400°. Combine the vinegar and shallots in a small heavy saucepan and bring to a boil. Reduce the heat slightly and simmer until the vinegar is reduced to about 2 tablespoons.

Add the butter and 1 tablespoon of the crème fraîche to the sauce. Set aside.

For the red snapper: Arrange the snapper fillets in a shallow baking dish, just large enough to hold them without overlapping. Pour the fish stock and the wine over the fillets. Season with salt and pepper and sit the dish on the middle rack of the oven. Bake for 8 to 10 minutes. The fish should be slightly underdone since it will continue cooking due to residual heat. Place the spinach on a serving platter. Arrange the baked fish on the spinach. Spoon the sauce over the fish. Garnish with lemon, lime and mint leaves.

*NOTE: The remaining crème fraîche can be kept in the refrigerator for up to 10 days. Use as a topping for fruits or desserts, if desired. (Raspberry vinegar may be purchased in gourmet or health food stores.)*

Yield: 2-4 servings

# *Alaska:*
## Governor Sarah Palin and First Gentleman Todd Palin

*Alaska has an estimated 100,000 glaciers which cover almost five percent of the state. There are more active glaciers in Alaska than in the rest of the inhabited world.*

## Pan Seared Salmon with Vegetable Asini Pepe

4 Salmon filets (6 oz.), deboned
1 c. Asini Pepe
1 medium zucchini, small dice
1 medium red pepper, small dice
1 corn (fresh on the cob), cut off the cob
1 medium carrot, small dice
½ medium red onion, small dice
Olive oil
Salt and pepper

Boil water and cook Asini Pepe. Drain. Mix with some oil and set aside. Sauté all vegetables together and add to Asini Pepe. Add olive oil to heated pan. Then add salmon to pan, flesh side down. Add salt and pepper to taste. Sear salmon until golden, approximately one minute on each side. Bake in 450˚ oven for 3 to 10 minutes, depending upon thickness. Serve on a bed of Asini Pepe.

## Hoisin Glazed Smoked Black Cod with Ginger Lemongrass Broth

For the fish:
4 (6-8 oz.) filets of smoked black cod (or halibut)
Hoisin sauce

For the broth:
2 cans chicken stock
1 stalk lemongrass, cut into 2 inch stalks
Fresh ginger (about 1 inch long, sliced)
1 T. fish sauce

For the salad:
1 small head of Napa cabbage, shredded
2 carrots, shredded
1 zucchini, shredded
½ bunch cilantro, rough chop
½ bunch scallions, chopped

To make the broth, simmer the broth with the fish sauce, ginger and lemongrass until the flavors infuse, about 20 minutes. Remove ginger and lemongrass and discard.
Pan sear fish in a hot sauté pan, flesh side down. When browned, turn over and spoon on one tablespoon of hoisin sauce on each filet. Put in 450˚ oven for 7 to 10 minutes or until fish is done. When fish is in the oven, add cabbage mixture into broth and heat until wilted, about 5 minutes. Serve in bowls adding the cabbage mixture first, then the broth and top with the fish.

# Arizona:

## Governor Janet Napolitano
## Given by: Mrs. John Rhodes, Wife of former Arizona Representative

*Arizona leads the nation in copper production.*
*The amount of copper on the roof of the Capitol building is equivalent to 4.8 million pennies.*
*The bolo tie is the official state neck-wear.*

## Brunch Casserole

16 slices white bread (sour dough), crust removed
8 slices cheese
5 slices bacon, cut up (or ham)
¼ c. green pepper, chopped
2 tsp. Worcestershire sauce
¼ lb. butter or margarine
6 eggs
½ tsp. salt
1 tsp. dry mustard

Place 8 slices of bread in 9 inch x 13 inch greased baking dish. Place on each slice the bacon or ham and cheese. Sprinkle green pepper over all. Place 8 slices of bread over this. Mix eggs and beat in rest of ingredients, except butter. Pour over bread and refrigerate overnight. Melt butter and drizzle over top. Bake at 350° for 1 hour.

Yield: 8 servings

# *Arkansas:*
## Governor Mike Beebe and First Lady Ginger Beebe
## Given by: Executive Chef Jason Knapp

*Arkansas has the only active diamond mine in the United States.*

*Alma, Arkansas is the "Spinach Capital of the World." The water tower is painted to represent the world's biggest can of spinach.*

## Governor's Mansion Rye Bread

*Governor's Mansion Rye Bread is served at most all dinners at the Governor's Mansion. Arkansas Tomato Corn Cake and Crab Napoleon was served to the Mansion Association. Grilled Mahi Mahi and Pomegranate Beurre Blanc was served at several state dinners. Strawberry Tart with Orange Cream was served at several private dinners.*

> 1 c. milk
> ½ c. shortening
> ¼ c. sugar
> 1 tsp. salt
> 1 T. yeast
> ¼ c. warm water (105 to 115°)
> 3 c. all-purpose flour
> 1 c. rye flour
> 3 large eggs, lightly beaten
> 1 tsp. vegetable oil
> 2 T. butter, melted

Heat first four ingredients in a saucepan until shortening melts, stirring occasionally. Cool to 105 to 115°.

Combine yeast and warm water in a 1 c. liquid measuring cup. Let stand 5 minutes. Sift white and wheat flour together.

Combine milk mixture, yeast mixture, 2 cups flour and eggs in a large bowl, stirring vigorously until mixture is blended. Add remaining two cups flour, stirring vigorously until dough pulls away from sides of bowl. Brush or lightly rub dough with vegetable oil. Cover loosely and let rise in a warm place (85°), free from drafts, 1 hour or until dough is doubled in bulk.

Grease 2 (8 ½ x 4 ½ x 3 inch) loaf pans. Set aside.

Punch dough down. Turn dough out onto a lightly floured surface and knead 3 minutes. Divide dough in half. Roll one portion of dough into a 12 x 8 ½ inch rectangle. Roll up dough, starting at short side, pressing firmly to eliminate air pockets. Pinch ends to seal. Place dough, seam side down, in a prepared pan. Repeat procedure with remaining portion of dough.

Brush loaves with melted butter. Cover loosely and let rise in a warm place, free from drafts, 1 hour or until dough almost reaches tops of pans.

Preheat oven to 350°. Bake for 30 to 40 minutes or until loaves sound hollow when tapped. Remove bread from pan immediately. Cool on wire racks.

Yield: 2 loaves

# Arkansas Tomato Corn Cake and Crab Napoleon

4 Arkansas Tomatoes, sliced thin
1 recipe corncakes
1 lb. jumbo lump crab (picked over)
1 c. citrus cream
1 avocado, sliced thin
½ c. Basil Oil
½ c. Balsamic Reduction
Salt and pepper taste

Corn Cake:
1 c. stone-ground yellow corn-meal (available at specialty food shops and many supermarkets)
½ c. all-purpose flour
1 tsp. salt
¾ tsp. baking soda
½ tsp. freshly ground pepper
2 tsp. sugar
2 T. unsalted butter, melted and cooled, plus additional melted butter for brushing the griddle
1 large egg
1 c. buttermilk

In a bowl, whisk together the corn-meal, flour, salt, baking soda, pepper and sugar. In a another bowl, whisk together 2 T. of butter, egg and but-termilk. Stir in the cornmeal mixture, stirring until the batter is just com-bined. Heat the griddle over moderately high heat until it is hot. Brush griddle lightly with the additional butter and working in batches drop the batter by heaping tablespoons onto the griddle. Spread batter slightly to form 1 ½ to 2 inch cakes. Cook cakes for 1 ½ to 2 minutes on each side or until they are golden, transferring them as they are cooked to a heat proof platter. Keep them warm.

Citrus Cream:
1 c. sour cream
2 tsp. lemon zest

Combine the zest into the sour cream. Chill.

Basil Oil:
2 c. fresh herbs (basil, thyme, cilantro, etc.)
1 ¾ c. canola oil
¼ c. extra virgin olive oil
½ tsp. salt

Boil the 2 cups of fresh herbs in water for 1 minute. Shock immediately. Heat canola oil and olive oil in pan until warm. Blend herbs and oils until smooth. Season with salt and strain.

Balsamic Reduction:
1 c. balsamic vinegar

Place into skillet and reduce by half.

Layering Process:
Begin by laying 1 slice tomato on plate, followed by 1 corn cake. Place ¼ cup crabmeat on corn cake and spread 1 T. citrus cream atop crabmeat. Repeat process twice more. Napoleon should stand 3 stacks high. Top with thinly sliced avocado. Drizzle with Basil Oil and Balsamic Reduction.

Yield: Serves 4

# Grilled Mahi Mahi with Pomegranate Beurre Blanc

1 Grilled Mahi Mahi Filet (works well with any firm white fish)

Pomegranate Beurre Blanc:
3 Shallots minced
1 tsp. black peppercorns
1 clove garlic, minced
1 bay leaf
1 ½ c. dry white wine
½ lb. unsalted butter, cut into ½ inch cubes
¾ c. pomegranate juice

Simmer the shallots, peppercorns, garlic, bay leaf and wine until reduced by ¾. Add the butter and incorporate into the wine reduction by stirring constantly, alternating on and off the heat. Add pomegranate juice until desired taste.

# Strawberry Tart with Orange Cream

1 rolled-out round of tart dough
8 oz. cream cheese at room temperature
½ c. sugar
1 tsp. finely grated orange zest
2 tsp. orange juice
2 tsp. Cointreau
2 c. fresh strawberries, hulled and halved lengthwise
½ c. orange marmalade

Fold the dough round in half and carefully transfer to a 9 ½ inch tart pan, preferably with a removable bottom.

Unfold and ease the round into the pan, without stretching it and pat it firmly into the bottom and up the sides of the pan. Trim off any excess dough by gently running a rolling pin across the top of the pan. Press the dough into the sides to extend it slightly above the rim to offset any shrinkage during baking.

Refrigerate or freeze the tart shell until firm, about 30 minutes. Meanwhile, position a rack in the lower third of an oven and preheat to 375°.

Line the pastry shell with aluminum foil or parchment paper and fill with pie weights or raw short-grain rice. Bake for 20 minutes, lift an edge of the foil. If the dough looks wet, continue to bake, checking every five minutes until the dough is pale gold (for a total baking time of 25 to 30 minutes). Remove the weights and foil. Continue to bake until the shell is golden, 7 to 10 minutes more. Transfer to a wire rack and let cool completely.

In the bowl of an electric mixer fitted with the flat beater, beat the cream cheese and sugar on medium speed until smooth. Mix in the orange zest, orange juice and Cointreau. Spread the cream cheese mixture evenly over the bottom of the tart shell. Arrange the strawberry halves, overlapping them, in concentric circles on top of the cream cheese, completely covering the surface.

In a small saucepan over low heat, warm the orange marmalade until it liquefies. Pour through a fine mesh strainer. Set over a small bowl. Using a small pastry brush, gently brush the strawberries with a thin coating of marmalade. Refrigerate until ready to serve. Let stand at room temperature for 20 minutes before serving.

# California:
## Governor Arnold Schwarzenegger and First Lady Maria Shriver

(*Schatzi recipe in* Famous Friends of the Wolf Cookbook)

*At Disneyland, every plant is edible in Tomorrowland. Guests are welcome to help themselves to bananas, strawberries, tomatoes and more.*

*The Golden Gate Bridge is so big that workers paint the bridge year round. It is time to begin repainting one end by the time they have finished the other end.*

## Maria's Oriental Chicken Salad

*This is one of First Lady Maria Shriver's favorite recipes.*

**Marinade for Chicken:**
1 c. low sodium soy sauce
3 oz. green onion chopped
1 ½ oz. ginger, peeled and julienned
2-3 oz. dark sesame oil
Salt and pepper to taste
2 lb. boneless chicken breasts

**Salad:**
¼ - ½ lb. mixed lettuce greens
1 head iceberg lettuce
1 bunch watercress, tops only
1 bunch cilantro
1 bunch mint, leaves only
1 large carrot
1 small cucumber
2 large oranges

**Sesame Rice Wine Vinaigrette:**
1 c. rice wine vinegar
½ c. peanut oil
½ c. sugar
2 T. dark sesame oil
1 T. low sodium soy sauce
Salt and pepper to taste
½ tsp. crushed red Chile pepper
½ c. toasted slivered almonds
1 pinch pickled ginger
Fried wonton skins for garnish

To prepare chicken, combine all marinade ingredients in a baking dish. Add salt and black pepper to taste. Place chicken breasts in the dish and refrigerate, preferably overnight. Preheat oven to 350°. Pour off and discard marinade. Bake chicken, skin side up for 30 minutes or until cooked through. Cool and remove skin. Shred chicken.

To prepare salad, clean lettuces and spin dry. Chill for crispness. Mix watercress, mint and cilantro with lettuce. Peel and julienne the carrot and cucumber. Peel and segment the oranges.

To prepare the vinaigrette, whisk all the ingredients together in a bowl.

To assemble salad, place all ingredients except wonton skins in a large mixing bowl. Dress lightly with vinaigrette and toss gently. Add more dressing as required. Garnish with crumbled wonton skins.

# Colorado:
## Governor Bill Ritter and First Lady Jeannie Ritter
## Given by: Mrs. Joel Hefley, Wife of Colorado Representative

*The World's First Rodeo was held on July 4th, 1869, in Deer Trail.*
*Katherine Lee Bates wrote "America the Beautiful" after being inspired by the view from Pikes Peak, Colorado.*

## Governor Ritter's Chocolate Cake

Cake:
¾ c. Hershey's cocoa
1 ½ tsp. baking soda
1 ½ c. hot water
2 c. sugar
1 c. safflower oil
2 c. flour
1 ½ tsp. baking powder
2 eggs (substitute egg beaters)
2 tsp. vanilla

Icing:
6 T. margarine, softened
½ c. Hershey's cocoa
2 ⅔ c. 10X sugar
⅓ c. skim milk
1 tsp. vanilla

Cake: Combine all ingredients for the cake. Spray a 13 x 9 inch pan with Pam. Fill with cake batter. Bake at 350° for 40 to 45 minutes.

Icing: Cream margarine in a bowl. Add cocoa and sugar alternately with milk. Blend in vanilla. Beat to spreading consistency.

# Connecticut:
## Governor M. Jodi Rell and First Gentleman Lou Rell

*Connecticut is home to the first hamburger (1895), Polaroid camera (1934), helicopter (1939), and color television (1948).*
*The first lollipop making machine opened for business in New Haven in 1908. George Smith named the treat after a popular race horse.*

## Apple Bars

1 stick of butter
1 c. of sugar
1 beaten egg
1 c. flour
1 c. diced apples
1 c. chopped walnuts
1 tsp. vanilla
½ tsp. cinnamon
¼ tsp. nutmeg
½ tsp. baking soda
½ tsp. baking powder
½ tsp. salt

Cream butter and sugar. Add egg. Sift dry ingredients. Add to mixture. Add apple, nuts and vanilla. Mix carefully, but fully. Pour into 8 x 8 inch greased pan and bake at 350° for about 40 minutes.

# Delaware:
## Governor Ruth Anne Minner

*Delaware has a state bug - the ladybug!*

*Horseshoe crabs may be viewed in large numbers up and down the Delaware shore in May. The crabs endure extremes of temperature and salinity. They can also go for a year without eating and have remained basically the same since the days of the dinosaur.*

## Governor Minner's Favorite Chicken Salad

*This is Governor Minner's favorite and a favorite of almost everyone else who eats at the Governor's Mansion!*

2 c. boiled chicken, diced
½ c. mayonnaise
½ c. celery, chopped
½ c. red onion, chopped
2 tsp. salad herbs
1 cube chicken buillon
1 stalk of celery
Dash of celery salt
Coarse pepper (to taste)

Boil the chicken with one stalk of celery, including leaves and one cube of chicken bullion. Chop ingredients and mix with chicken.

# Florida:
## Governor Charlie Crist

*Gatorade was named for the University of Florida Gators where the drink was first developed.*

## Governor's Favorite Key Lime Pie

Filling:
½ c. fresh Key Lime lime juice
(you can use any fresh lime juice if necessary)
4 tsp. grated lime zest
4 egg yolks
1 (14 oz.) can sweetened condensed milk

Pie Crust:
11 graham crackers
3 T. granulated sugar
5 T. unsalted butter, melted
(Can be substituted with a ready made graham cracker pie crust)

Whisk the egg yolks and lime zest together in a bowl until tinted light green. This takes about two minutes. Beat in milk, then juice and set aside until it thickens. Preheat oven to 325˚.
Process graham crackers in food processor or blender. Mix graham cracker crumbs and sugar in another bowl. Add butter and stir with fork until well blended. Pour into 9 inch pie pan and press firmly over bottom and up sides of pan.
Bake pie crust on center rack or until crust is light brown and then cool to room temperature.
Pour lime filling into crust, spread evenly. Bake for 15 minutes until the center sets, but still wiggles when shaken. Remove from oven and allow to cool to room temperature. Refrigerate until thoroughly cool and enjoy!

# Georgia:
## Governor Sonny Perdue and First Lady Mary Perdue

*In Gainesville, the Chicken Capital of the World, it is illegal to eat chicken with a fork. Known as the sweetest onion in the world, the Vidalia onion can only be grown in the fields around Vidalia and Glennville.*

## Crab Chowder

¼ tsp. minced garlic
⅛ tsp. cayenne
¼ c. green peppers
1 T. butter
2 cans potato soup
1 (8 oz.) package cream cheese
1 ½ cans of milk
6+ oz. crabmeat
Chopped onions
1 can whole kernel corn
⅛ c. sugar

Cook onions, garlic, peppers and cayenne in butter. Blend soup, cream cheese, and milk. Add crabmeat. Add undrained corn. Bring to boil. Reduce heat. Simmer for 10 minutes. Stir in sugar.

Yield: 6-8 servings

# Guam:
## Governor Felix Camacho and First Lady Joann Camacho

*The roads on the island of Guam are made with coral. Guam has no sand. The sand on the beaches is actually ground coral. When concrete is mixed, the coral sand is used instead of importing regular sand from thousands of miles away.*

# Macaroon Kiss Cookies

⅓ c. unsalted butter, softened
1 (3 oz.) package cream cheese, softened
¾ c. sugar
1 egg yolk
2 tsp. almond extract
2 tsp. orange juice
1 ¼ c. all-purpose flour, unsifted
2 tsp. baking powder
¼ tsp. salt
5 c. flaked coconut (14 oz. package)
1 (9 oz.) package Hershey's Kisses candies, unwrapped

Cream butter, cream cheese and sugar in a large mixing bowl until light and fluffy. Add egg yolk, almond extract and orange juice. Beat well. Combine flour, baking powder and salt. Gradually add to creamed mixture. Stir in 3 cups of flaked coconut. Cover tightly. Chill 1 hour or until firm enough to handle. Shape dough in 1 inch balls and roll in remaining coconut. Place 8 balls on each ungreased cookie sheet.
Bake at 350˚ for 13 to 15 minutes or until lightly browned. Remove from oven. Immediately press unwrapped Hershey's Kisses on top of each cookie. Cool for one minute. Carefully remove from cookie sheet. Cool completely on wire rack.

Yield: Approximately 3 dozen cookies

# Hawaii:
## Governor Linda Lingle
## Given by: Executive Chef of Washington Place, Alan Awana

*More than one-third of the world's commercial supply of pineapples comes from Hawaii.*
*The Hawaiian Islands are the projecting tops of the biggest mountain range in the world.*

## Governor's Snicker Fudge Brownie with Pan Roasted Macadamia Nuts

1 box fudge brownie mix (any brand)
½ c. pan roasted Macadamia Nuts, chopped
Chopped Walnuts may be used in place of Macadamia Nuts
¼ c. Swiss Milk chocolate morsels
1 king size Snicker's bar
1 medium scoop Vanilla Ice cream, optional
Raspberries, garnish

Chop nuts (coarse) and pan roast on medium high. Roast until almost completely blackened. Set aside to cool. Cut snicker's bar in half lengthwise and then cut into ½ inch morsels. Follow brownie mix directions. Add the Swiss Milk morsels and ½ of the nuts and snickers. Pour into 3 ½ inch x 3 inch deep ramekin. Coat with non-stick spray and flour before adding mix. Bake accordingly. However, cut baking time by 5 minutes, but do not remove from oven. Open oven and add snicker morsels and other ½ of nuts evenly over top of brownies. Close oven for 2 minutes then remove. Morsels should be almost completely melted. Times may vary due to different ovens.

Optional:
After cooling for about 20 minutes remove from ramekin. Cut a circle into the center of the brownie about the size of a 50 cent piece and remove. Hold cut out. Dust a dessert plate with confectioners' sugar, place brownie in center and add a large scoop of vanilla ice cream to center of brownie. Top with a dusting of confectioners' sugar and a sprig of mint. Add some fresh raspberries to garnish plate.

Yield: 6 servings

# Asparagus–Cucumber Veggie Wrap

2 lbs. Asparagus (stalks peeled, ends cut)
1 medium cucumber, striped, seeded, and julienne
1 bunch chickory or other lettuce shredded
3 pcs. Stuffer or favorite mushroom thinly sliced
1-2 medium tomato, seeded and cubed- set aside
4 oz. clover or alfalfa sprouts
¾ c. Ranch dressing
4-6 slices bacon, cut fine and cooked crisp- oil removed
6-8 flour tortilla or burrito wrappers
1 stalk celery, minced fine
2 large avocados (sliced to 16 equal pieces)
¼ c. extra-light olive oil
¼ basil, minced fine

Dressing:
Mix Ranch dressing, celery and bacon together and set aside.

Veggies:
Toss all ingredients with dressing in large bowl except for tomato, asparagus and avocado. Combine olive oil and basil with tomato.

Wraps:
Evenly divide asparagus on all the wraps with the tips extending out on both ends. Top with equal portions of veggie mixture. Complete this step with 2 to 3 slices of avocado across top of mixture. Roll wrap so end is on bottom.

Slice in center and lean one piece over the other. Evenly drizzle the tomato mixture over the top of wraps. Serve immediately.

Yield: 8 servings

*Note: All ingredients may be substituted based on availability.*

# Idaho:
## Governor CL "Butch" Otter and First Lady Lori Otter

*Sun Valley is recognized as the home of America's first destination ski resort. Nearly all of the potatoes grown within the borders of the state of Idaho used to be one variety, the Russet Burbank. Henry Spaulding planted the first potatoes in Idaho. His first potato crop was planted near Lapwai, Idaho in 1837.*

## The Best Meatloaf Ever!

1 lb. ground beef
1 egg (slightly beaten)
¾ c. quick cooking oatmeal
1 T. dried onion, minced

Sauce:
15-16 oz. tomato sauce (1 med. can)
½ c. brown sugar
4 tsp. prepared mustard
3 slices raw bacon

Place ground beef and oatmeal in a bowl and mix together until all oatmeal is incorporated.

Add onion and mix again. Set aside for at least 5 minutes. Meanwhile, in a separate bowl, mix tomato sauce, brown sugar and mustard until color is even. (If preparing ahead, store meat mixture and sauce separately until ready to cook.)

Break egg and pour over ground beef and mix together. Add half of sauce to meat and mix thoroughly. (This meatloaf is soft and juicy when unbaked, but firms up when cooked.)

Form meat into loaf about one inch smaller all directions than dish to be cooked in. Place loaf in center of Dutch oven liner pan. Pour about a third of the remaining sauce over the meat. Place bacon strips over the sauce. Cover with remaining sauce. (Note: The sauce should coat the loaf, with the extra sauce settling to the bottom of the pan.)

Assemble Dutch oven by placing coals both on top of lid and under bottom of oven. Start with about 8-10 coals under the oven and about 15-20 on the top of the oven. (If cooking indoors, merely place liner pan in oven.)

Bake in Dutch oven for one hour at 350˚. If making multiple recipes, increase cooking time. The best way to tell when the loaf is finished is by texture and temperature, as the meat will retain a slight red tinge from the sauce even when cooked.

*Note: One recipe makes 4-6 servings. However, I recommend making two recipes at a time to allow leftovers for sandwiches. Two recipes make enough to feed 3-4 people 2 meals each. While most kids seem to not like regular meatloaf, all children seem to all love this one. This recipe gets rave reviews every time! Great for outdoor cooking and camping trips! Enjoy!!!*

Yield: 4-6 servings

# Turkey Noodle Bake

8 oz. wide egg noodles, cooked as package directs
2 ½ c. milk
3 T. flour
1 T. Wyler's Chicken-Flavor Bouillon Granules or 3 cubes
½ c. sour cream or plain yogurt
2 c. cubed cooked turkey
1 pkg. (10 oz.) frozen chopped broccoli thawed
1 c. (4 oz.) shredded Cheddar cheese

Preheat oven to 375˚. In medium saucepan, combine milk, flour and bouillon and stir until flour is dissolved. Cook over medium heat, stirring, until slightly thickened.

In large bowl, combine all ingredients except cheese. Coat a 2 quart baking dish with vegetable cooking spray and spoon the mixture into dish. Top with cheese.

Cover and bake for 25 to 30 minutes or until hot and bubbly. Delicious! Nice way to serve leftover Christmas or Thanksgiving turkey.

Yield: 4 servings

# Illinois:
## Governor Rod Blagojevich and First Lady Patricia Blagojevich

*In 1885, the world's first Skyscraper was built in Chicago.*
*The Chicago Post Office at 433 West Van Buren is the only postal facility in the world you can drive a car through.*

# Chicken Salad

1 lb. chicken cubed
¼ tsp. granulated garlic
⅛ c. Italian dressing
1 c. Miracle Whip
2 T. Parmesan Cheese
1 c. red or green grapes
Salt and pepper (to taste)

Combine all the ingredients except for salt and pepper. Serve as a sandwich or on mixed greens with garden fresh tomatoes.

# *Indiana:*
## Governor Mitch Daniels and First Lady Cheri Daniels

*Santa Claus, Indiana, receives more than one-half million letters and requests at Christmas time.*

## "Straw and Hay" Pasta (Paglia Fieno)

*This is a dish that my family loves and a favorite of many of our guests. It feeds a crowd and freezes well!*

> 12 T. butter or margarine, divided
> 1 clove garlic, minced
> 1 ½ lbs. Italian sausage removed from casings and crumbled (or bulk)
> 4 ½ tsp. minced parsley
> 1 tsp. dried basil or 4 fresh basil leaves, minced
> Generous dash of tarragon
> Dash each of thyme, oregano, sage, and nutmeg
> Salt and pepper (to taste)
> 1 ½ lbs. mushrooms, sliced
> 1 lb. each green and white pasta (spaghetti or linguini)
> 1 ½ c. heavy cream
> ½ c. grated Parmesan cheese

In a large deep skillet or Dutch oven, melt 10 tablespoons butter. Add garlic. Cook until golden brown. Add sausage, parsley, and seasonings. Cook 20 minutes. Stir frequently. Add mushrooms. Cook 15 minutes longer. Keep hot. In a very large kettle, cook pasta following package directions. Drain. In same kettle, melt remaining 2 tablespoons butter. Add pasta. Sauté lightly over low heat. Add half the sausage mixture and all the cream. Toss well over medium heat until cream thickens slightly (no more than 3 minutes). Transfer to platter. Top with remaining sausage mixture. Serve at once with Parmesan.

Yield: 6-8 servings

# Iowa:
## Governor Chet Culver and First Lady Mari Thinnes Culver
## Given by: Executive Chef Sharon Van Verth

*Strawberry Point is the home of the world's largest strawberry.*
*Quaker Oats, in Cedar Rapids, is the largest cereal company in the world.*

## Pork Tenderloin on Cocktail Roll Served with Corn Relish

2 pork tenderloins, about 1 lb. each
2 cloves garlic, peeled and cut into slivers
2 T. Tone's Steak Seasoning or your choice of steak seasoning
1 T. Tone's dried rosemary, crushed or your choice of rosemary
1 tsp. Tone's dried thyme or your choice of thyme
3 T. extra-virgin olive oil
2 T. brandy
½ c. reduced salt chicken broth

Corn Relish:
4 ears of "Iowa Fresh" Corn on the cob
1 small red onion
3 T. Rhubarb Jam
½ jalapeno, finely diced

Preheat oven to 350˚. With the tip of a sharp knife, make deep little slits all over the tenderloin and insert the garlic slivers. Mix the seasonings and olive oil to-gether in a small bowl. Rub the mixture over the tenderloins.

Heat a skillet and sear the tenderloins well on medium high heat for approximately 10 minutes. Place the tenderloins in the oven and cook approximately 10 minutes. Remove and let rest.

Deglaze the pan with brandy and chicken broth. Reheat at serving time. Slice pork thinly and place on platter and pour the brandy and chicken broth over meat. Serve with small cocktail roll and the corn relish. Cut the corn off the cob and mix the remainder ingredients.

Yield: Depending on thickness of cut, this should serve approximately 16

# Kansas:
## Governor Kathleen Sebelius and First Gentleman Gary Sebelius

*At one time it was against the law to serve ice cream on cherry pie in Kansas. In 1990, Kansas wheat farmers produced enough wheat to make 33 billion loaves of bread or enough to provide each person on earth with 6 loaves.*

## Decadent Chocolate Cake

1 c. boiling water
3 oz. unsweetened chocolate
8 T. (1 stick) sweet butter
1 tsp. vanilla extract
2 c. granulated sugar
2 eggs separated
1 tsp. baking soda
½ c. dairy sour cream
2 c. less 2 T. unbleached, all-purpose flour, sifted
1 tsp. baking powder
Chocolate Frosting (recipe follows)

Preheat oven to 350˚. Grease and flour a 10 inch tube pan. Knock out excess. Pour boiling water over chocolate and butter. Let stand until melted. Stir vanilla and sugar, then whisk in egg yolks, one at a time, blending well after each addition. Mix baking soda and sour cream and whisk into chocolate mixture. Sift flour and baking powder together and add to batter, mixing thoroughly. Beat egg whites until stiff but not dry. Stir a quarter of the egg whites thoroughly into the batter.

Scoop remaining egg whites on top of the batter and gently fold together. Pour batter into the prepared pan. Set on the middle rack of the oven and bake for 40 to 50 minutes or until the edges have pulled away from the sides of the pan and a cake tester inserted into the center comes out clean. Cool in pan for 10 minutes. Unmold and cool completely before frosting.

Yield: 12 portions

## Chocolate Frosting:

2 T. sweet butter
¾ c. semisweet chocolate chips
6 T. heavy cream
1 ¼ c. sifted confectioners' sugar, or as needed
1 tsp. vanilla extract

Place all ingredients in a heavy saucepan over low heat and whisk until smooth. Cool slightly. Add more sugar if necessary.

## Zucchini Frittata

*Good for brunch or tailgates...*

1 ½ c. chopped onion
2-3 T. butter or best-quality olive oil
½ lb. zucchini, peeled and shredded
12 eggs, beaten
2 T. fresh basil or 2 tsp. dried
2 tsp. salt
Cracked pepper to taste
3 T. dry bread crumbs
2 cloves garlic, minced (optional)
2 tomatoes, peeled and sliced
1 c. grated Cheddar cheese
½ c. grated Parmesan cheese

Sauté onion in butter or oil. Add zucchini and cook about 2 minutes. To beaten eggs, add basil, salt and pepper. Fold in onion-zucchini mixture, bread crumbs and garlic, if desired. Pour into buttered quiche dish. Arrange tomatoes on top and sprinkle with Cheddar and Parmesan cheese. Bake at 350° for 20-25 minutes or until set.

Yield: 6 servings as an entrée and 12 servings as a first course

## Broccoli and Cherry Tomatoes

1 large bunch broccoli
¼ c. butter
3 T. fresh lemon juice
½ tsp. basil
½ pt. cherry tomatoes, sliced in half
Salt and freshly ground pepper (to taste)

Steam broccoli until tender-crisp. Rinse under cold water, pat dry and cut into small florets. (This may be done early in the day.) Melt butter. Add lemon juice and basil. Put broccoli into a skillet over high heat and pour lemon butter over it. Toss it for 1-2 minutes. Add cherry tomatoes, salt and pepper and toss briefly. Serve immediately. Easy and pretty holiday vegetable. You may substitute green beans for broccoli.

Yield: 4-6 servings

# White Bean Salad with Shrimp and Asparagus

*Good summer salad...*

2 c. (1 inch) sliced asparagus (about ½ lb.)
¾ lb. medium shrimp, peeled and deveined
½ tsp. freshly ground black pepper, divided
¼ tsp. salt, divided
1 tsp. vegetable oil
2 c. torn spinach
1 (19 oz.) can cannellini beans, drained and rinsed
3 bacon slices
½ c. chopped Vidalia green onions
1 garlic clove, minced
¼ c. fat-free, less sodium chicken broth
1 T. fresh parsley, chopped
2 T. fresh lemon juice
1 T. cider vinegar

Steam asparagus, covered, for 3 minutes. Drain and rinse with cold water. Sprinkle shrimp with ⅛ teaspoon pepper and ⅛ teaspoon salt. Heat oil in a medium nonstick skillet over medium high heat. Add shrimp; sauté 4 minutes. Remove from pan. Place in a large bowl. Add asparagus, spinach and beans to shrimp. Toss well. Add bacon to pan. Cook over medium heat until crisp. Remove bacon from pan and crumble. Reserve 2 teaspoons drippings in pan. Add onions and garlic, cook 3 minutes, stirring frequently. Remove from heat. Add remaining pepper, ⅛ teaspoon salt, bacon, broth and the remaining ingredients. Drizzle dressing over salad. Toss to coat. Serve immediately.

Yield: 4 Servings

# *Kentucky:*
## Governor Steven Beshear and First Lady Jane Beshear

*Cheeseburgers were first served in 1934 at Kaelin's in Louisville.*
*"Happy Birthday to You" was the creation of two Louisville sisters in 1893.*

## Kentucky Hot Brown

*All three recipes are traditional Kentucky fare!*

3 oz. turkey breast, roasted, sliced
2 slices toasted white bread
2 slices tomato
2 slices bacon, cooked and drained

Sauce:
2 oz. butter
3 oz. flour
1 c. milk
½ c. Cheddar cheese, grated
Salt and white pepper (to taste)

Heat butter and add flour. Whisk and slowly cook for 3 minutes. Whisk in milk and heat until thick. Whisk in cheese until melted. Season.
Place toast in an oven safe dish. Add turkey. Cover well with sauce. Top with tomatoes then bacon. Bake at 400° for 10 minutes.

# Corn Pudding

3 c. corn
6 eggs, lightly beaten
3 c. heavy cream
½ c. sugar
1 tsp. sugar
1 tsp. flour
½ tsp. baking powder
2 tsp. butter

Blend dry ingredients together. Stir eggs and heavy cream together. Add dry ingredients and butter blending well. Add corn. Pour into greased casserole and bake at 350° for 1 hour until firm and golden brown.

Yield: 10 servings

# Chocolate Bourbon Pudding Cakes

1 ½ c. butter
¾ c. water
12 oz. semi-sweet chocolate, chopped
1 ½ c. sugar
3 T. bourbon
1 ½ T. vanilla
6 large eggs

Combine butter, water and chocolate in small saucepan and simmer over low heat until chocolate is melted. Set aside until cool. Stir in bourbon and vanilla. Add eggs one at a time until completely incorporated. Pour into six 8 ounce glass ramekins. Bake at 325° for 20 minutes. Allow to cool slightly and turn onto dessert plate. Serve with sprinkling of powdered sugar on top and your favorite vanilla ice cream.

# Louisiana:
## Governor Bobby Jindal and First Lady Supriya Jindal
## Given by: Junior League of Lake Charles, Louisiana (Pirate's Pantry)

*Louisiana was named in honor of King Louis XIV.*

*Louisiana has the tallest state capitol building in the United States. The building is 450 feet tall with 34 floors.*

*Louisiana is the only state in the union that does not have counties. Its political subdivisions are called parishes.*

*Milk was adopted as the official drink of Louisiana in 1983.*

# Bayou Hush Puppies

1 c. boiling water
1 c. yellow cornmeal
2 tsp. salt
1 small onion, finely chopped
1 egg, slightly beaten
Flour

Bring the water to a boil in a saucepan. Combine the meal and salt. Add gradually to the boiling water, stirring constantly. Remove from the heat and stir to a smooth, thick mush and cool. Add the onion and egg. Mix thoroughly. Form the mixture into small balls, roll in flour and fry with fish.

Yield: About 20 servings

# Maine:
## Governor John Baldacci and First Lady Karen Baldacci

*More blueberries are grown in Maine than any other state.*
*Maine lobsters have won international fame for their flavor and contribution to the culinary world.*

## Lazy Lobster

*Lazy Lobster and Curried Buttermilk Squash Soup were served at the Blaine House for lunch when the governor's office transitioned from the Angus S. King administration to the John E. Baldacci administration.*

> 4 Maine Lobsters
> ½ c. melted butter with a lemon twist
> 8 lemon wedges

Cook the lobsters to slightly undone in boiling water for 20 minutes. Remove the lobsters from the pot and let them cool enough to handle. Remove the claws, but leave the rest of each lobster intact. Turn each lobster on its back and take a very sharp knife or a pair of good kitchen scissors and cut the shell in the middle from the tail to the body. You will want to trim the under shell back to the red top. Remove the tail meat and drain as much of the liquid as you can. Cut the meat into bite size pieces and return to the laid back lobster which should be on a jelly roll pan or a roaster. Now take out the claw meat. Be very careful to keep the claw meat intact and add the knuckle meat to the tail meat and whatever other bits of meat you have. Now use your beautiful claw meat on top. Melt some butter and a squeeze of lemon and drizzle over each laid back lobster. Before serving, cover your pan tightly with foil before putting the lobster in the oven at 420° for 10 minutes if they have been refrigerated and prepared early. If you have just prepared the Lazy Lobster, cook for only 5 minutes.

When you do plate the Lazy Lobster, place a lemon wedge on each side of the lobster to prevent it from rolling on the plate.

This is a nice way to serve lobster without the guests having to take it apart at the dinner table.

# Curried Butternut Squash Soup

6 T. butter
3 medium onions chopped
1 8 oz. celery, chopped
1 lb. of carrots, shredded
3 medium butternut squash, peeled, seeded and cubed
1 clove garlic, minced
2 (49 ½ oz.) cans of chicken or vegetable broth
1 T. curry powder
Salt and pepper (to taste)

Melt butter, sauté onions, celery, carrots and garlic until soft. Add squash, stock, curry, salt and pepper. Bring to a boil and then simmer until squash is tender. Puree in food processor or blender. Remove and strain for a velvety soup. For presentation serve the soup with a dollop of sour cream or yogurt and add a small sprig of parsley for accent.

Yield: 16 servings

# Maryland:
## Governor Martin O'Malley and First Lady Katie O'Malley
## Given by: Head Chef Medford Canby, Government House of Maryland

*America's first umbrellas were produced in Baltimore, beginning in 1828. America's national anthem was written by Francis Scott Key, a Maryland lawyer. It is believed that Key wrote the anthem on September 14, 1814, while watching the bombardment of Fort McHenry in Baltimore Harbor.*

# Rockfish with Crab Sauce

*This is a favorite recipe from our residence's kitchen. My family really enjoys this dish by Chef Medford.*

Rockfish:
4-6 oz. pieces Rockfish Filet

Sprinkle each piece of fish with salt and pepper. Dust with a little flour. Sauté in 2 tablespoons clarified butter or oil on medium heat for about 3 minutes per side until golden.

Crab Sauce:
1 lb. jumbo lump crabmeat
2 T. lemon juice
4 T. olive oil
2 tsp. capers
2 tsp. anchovy paste
1 T. chives, chopped
½ tsp. salt
¼ tsp. pepper

Sauté crabmeat until hot. In a separate bowl, whisk together rest of ingredients. Add hot crabmeat and spoon over fish.

# Massachusetts:
## Governor Deval Patrick and First Lady Diane Patrick

*Boston built the first subway system in the United States in 1897.*
*Norfolk County is the birthplace of four United States presidents: John Adams, John Quincy Adams, John Fitzgerald Kennedy and George Herbert Walker Bush.*
*The first Thanksgiving Day was celebrated in Plymouth in 1621.*

## Bouillabaisse

*This is Governor Patrick's personal recipe. It's tomato-based, like Cioppino.*

Base:
½ c. olive oil
1 c. chopped onions
½ small fennel bulb, chopped (or ½ tsp. seeds)
4 garlic cloves, sliced
2 c. chopped plum tomatoes
6 sprigs Italian parsley
3 sprigs fresh thyme (or ½ tsp. dried)
1 bay leaf
¼ tsp. crumbled saffron
Piece of orange peel
6 c. water
2 c. clam juice
1 fish head (optional)
Shrimp shell (optional)
Salt and pepper

Stew:
4 potatoes, peeled and sliced
1 ½ lbs. cod, haddock, halibut or monkfish
1 ½ lbs. flounder, sole or schrod
2 small lobsters cut into 8 pieces each (or 1 lb. lobster meat)
½ lb. shrimp, shelled
½ lb. scallops
1 doz. mussels
1 doz. Little Necks

Rouille:
½ c. fresh breadcrumbs
2 dry chili peppers, seeded, soaked for 10 minutes and chopped
5 cloves garlic
½ c. olive oil
3-4 T. bouillabaisse broth

In a stockpot, heat oil and sauté onions for 2 minutes. Add fennel, garlic and tomatoes and cook for 2 minutes.
Add parsley, thyme, bay leaf, saffron, orange peel, clam juice, water and fish head. Boil for 20 minutes. Strain and season with salt and pepper.
Bring strained broth to a boil and add potatoes and firmer fish. Simmer 10 minutes. Add lean fish, lobster, shrimp, scallops, mussels and clams. Cook 10 minutes (discard any shellfish that haven't opened).
Make rouille: dampen bread crumbs with water and process with all the other rouille ingredients. Serve with French bread toasts spread with rouille.

# Michigan:
## Governor Jennifer M. Granholm and First Gentleman Daniel Granholm Mulhern
## Given by: Executive Chef Scott Hershey

*Celery was first grown in the United States in the 1850s by Dutch settlers in Kalmazoo, Michigan.*

*The Kellogg Company has made Battle Creek the Cereal Capital of the World. The Kellogg brothers accidentally discovered the process for producing flaked cereal products and sparked the beginning of the dry cereal industry. Battle Creek, Michigan, is sometimes referred to as "Cereal City." It is home to major cereal producers Kellogg and Post.*

## Banana Foster's Bread Pudding

    1 ½ each Texas toast loaves,
    stale and cubed
    10 eggs
    2 qt. half & half
    5 c. granulated sugar
    3 T. vanilla extract
    1 T. almond extract
    6 oz. dark rum
    6 oz. banana liqueur
    6 oz. butterscotch schnapps
    (optional)
    4 Bananas, puree – use spotted
    and very ripened banana
    3 c. dried cherries, soaked in rum
    1 ½ c. white chocolate chips
    (optional)

Whisk eggs with next 8 ingredients to make custard. Combine custard with bread and cherries. Mix ingredients well and let rest 2 hours or overnight until bread has absorbed custard. Spray two 9 x 13 inch pans with oil. Pour batter evenly between them and cover with foil. Bake in a preheated 350° oven for approximately 45 minutes. Remove foil and continue baking until custard has set, approximately 20 minutes longer. Let rest 10 minutes before serving.

*Optional: After batter has rested and just before baking, fold in white chocolate chips.*
*Serving suggestions: custard sauce, caramel sauce or fruit puree.*

Yield: Two 9 x 13 inch dishes

# *Minnesota:*
## Governor Tim Pawlenty and First Lady Mary Pawlenty

*Minnesotan baseball commentator Halsey Hal was the first to say 'Holy Cow' during a baseball broadcast. Minneapolis is home to the oldest continuously running theater (Old Log Theater) and the largest dinner theater (Chanhassen Dinner Theater) in the country.*

*Minnesota has 90,000 miles of shoreline, more than California, Florida and Hawaii combined.*

## Victorian Raspberry French Toast

> 6 large eggs
> 2 tsp. vanilla extract
> Pinch of salt
> 2 ½ c. half and half
> ¾ c. sugar
> 12 oz. cream cheese
> ¾ tsp. ground nutmeg
> 10 croissants, diced into 1 ½ inch pieces
> 8 oz. fresh raspberries
> 1 ½ c. pure maple syrup
> 4 (10 oz.) casserole dishes, greased
> Powdered sugar

Preheat oven to 275˚. Mix together cream cheese, ¼ cup sugar, ¼ teaspoon nutmeg until smooth. Add to diced croissants in 1 teaspoon pieces. Toss so that cream cheese is randomly dispersed throughout.

Beat together eggs, vanilla, salt, cream, ½ cup sugar, ½ teaspoon nutmeg to make custard and pour over croissant mixture. Add raspberries. Toss and allow to soak for 3 minutes.

Pour 2 ounces maple syrup in each casserole bottom, and fill casseroles with croissant mixture to rim. Top off with remaining custard and cook in oven for approximately 40 minutes or until center of casserole is golden brown and firm to the touch. Drizzle with remaining maple syrup and dust with powdered sugar.

# Mississippi:

## Governor Haley Barbour and First Lady Marsha Barbour Given by: Chef Luis Bruno, Mississippi Governor's Mansion

*In 1884, the concept of selling shoes in pairs by the box (right foot and left foot) occurred in Vicksburg at Phil Gilbert's Shoe Parlor on Washington Street. Root beer was invented in Biloxi in 1898 by Edward Adolf Barq, Sr.*

## Crab Louie

*This is served as a luncheon salad or as an appetizer at dinners and receptions at the Mississippi Governor's Mansion by Chef Luis Bruno.*

> 2 c. lump crabmeat (1 lb.)
> 1 c. Hellman's mayonnaise
> 4 tsp. chili sauce
> 1 quarter red bell pepper, sliced
> 1 whole freshly squeezed lemon juice
> 1 small bunch scallions, finely chopped
> 1 hard boiled egg, diced
> 1 tomato, seeded and diced
> 1 avocado; seeded, peeled, and diced
> Worcestershire (to taste)
> Hot sauce (to taste)
> Salt and pepper (to taste)
> Any desired lettuce (Bibb, baby greens, etc)

Carefully pick through the crab and discard any bits of shell. Try to leave lumps intact as much as possible. Place meat in a bowl.

In another medium bowl, whisk together the mayonnaise, chili sauce, lemon juice, Worcestershire, hot sauce and salt and pepper to taste.

Gently fold remaining items in your crab bowl: red pepper, scallions, egg, tomatoes, avocado and ½ cup of dressing (salt and pepper to taste or as needed). Toss lettuce with ¼ cup dressing (optional). Divide among four plates and add Crab Louie on top of lettuce. Great with seasoned crostini as an appetizer.

# *Missouri:*
## Governor Matt Blunt and First Lady Melanie Blunt

*The ice cream cone was invented at the St. Louis World's Fair in 1904 when an ice cream vendor ran out of cups and asked a waffle vendor to help by rolling up waffles to hold ice cream.*

*The first ready-mix food to be sold commercially was Aunt Jemima pancake flour. It was invented in St. Joseph, Missouri and introduced in 1899.*

## Grasshoppers

*This recipe is one of Mrs. Blunt's favorites from Sassafras: The Ozarks Cookbook, from the Junior League of Springfield. Mrs. Blunt has used this recipe for afternoon teas and coffees at the Governor's Mansion.*

*A luscious combination of chocolate and peppermint…*

4 eggs
2 c. sugar
1 c. cocoa
1 c. flour
1 tsp. peppermint extract
1 c. butter, melted

Frosting:
3 ½ c. powdered sugar (1 pound)
½ c. butter
3 drops green food coloring
½ tsp. peppermint extract
1 to 2 T. milk
3 oz. unsweetened chocolate
3 T. butter

Preheat oven to 350˚. Grease and flour an 11 x 17 inch pan. In a large mixing bowl, beat eggs and sugar until thick. Add cocoa, flour and peppermint extract. Stir in butter. Pour into prepared pan. Bake 15-20 minutes, being careful not to over bake. Let cool.

To prepare frosting, cream powdered sugar, butter, food coloring and peppermint extract. Add milk to spreading consistency. Spread over cooled cake. Melt chocolate and butter on the top of a double boiler or in a microwave. Carefully brush over frosted cake. Refrigerate to harden. Cut into 1 x 2 inch bars.

Yield: 7-8 dozen

# Montana:
Governor Brian Schweitzer and First Lady Nancy Schweitzer
Given by: Chef and Resident Manager Jane Brophy

*Montana's rivers and streams provide water for three oceans and three of the North American continent's major river basins. The largest snowflake ever observed was 38 centimeters wide was recorded in Montana on January 28, 1887. That's nearly 15 inches. Amazing!*

## Ginger Dressing

1 c. canola oil
1 ½ oz. fresh ginger
1 ½ oz. chopped onion
1 oz. celery, sliced
½ tsp. honey
¼ c. toasted sesame seeds
Pinch white pepper
Pinch celery seeds
½ tsp. catsup
⅓ c. tamari
⅓ c. white vinegar

Using food processor, mix all ingredients together, except oil, until well blended. Add oil slowly with machine running. Chill. Great on green salad, as well as chicken, rice and vegetables.

# Nebraska:
Governor Dave Heineman and First Lady Sally Ganem

*Kool-Aid was invented by Edwin Perkins in 1927 in Hastings. He changed his soft drink syrup, Fruit Smack, into a powder to make it easier to ship. Nebraska is the only state in the union with a unicameral (one house) legislature.*

## Dinner Rolls

*The Nebraska Governor's Residence hosts many luncheons for civic and state organizations. Kathy, their chef, bakes the rolls for all these events as well as for dinner parties hosted by Governor Heineman and First Lady Ganem. No matter how scrumptious the meal, it's always the rolls that receive the great reviews.*

2 c. flour
½ c. sugar
⅓ c. powdered milk
1 tsp. salt
1 T. yeast

Mix together with spoon.

1 c. water
1 c. milk (or half and half)
⅓ c. Fleishman's margarine

Microwave second set of ingredients 1 ½ minutes on full power (margarine may not be melted entirely, that is okay.) Add to dry ingredients and mix 2 minutes. Add 3 – 3 ½ cups more flour (Dough satiny but sticky.)

Use dough hook to make rolls. Let dough rise until doubled. Punch down. Let rise until ½ doubled. Punch down. Let rest 5 minutes. Form rolls. Let double. Bake for 5 minutes. Turn oven down to 350˚ for 12 to 15 minutes, until nicely browned.

# Nevada:
## Governor Jim Gibbons and First Lady Dawn Gibbons

*Frank Sinatra once owned the Cal-Neva at Lake Tahoe's Crystal Bay. It is possible to stand in both Nevada and California inside Cal-Neva's building.*
*Shrimp consumption in Las Vegas is more than 60,000 pounds a day -- higher than the rest of the country combined! About 150 couples get married in Las Vegas each day.*

## Fried Green Tomatoes

- 4 medium green tomatoes
- 1 c. bread crumbs
- 2 eggs
- ½ c. Parmesan cheese
- 1 c. cooking oil

Cut unpeeled tomatoes into ½ inch slices. Beat the eggs in a small bowl. Dip the tomato slices in the egg first. Then dip the slices into crushed bread crumbs. Heat the cooking oil in a frying pan. Cook battered tomato slices in oil until the sides are brown. Drain off excess oil in a paper towel. Place slices on a dish and sprinkle with Parmesan cheese.

Yield: 4 servings

## Nevada Sugar Cookies

- 1 ½ c. sugar
- ⅔ c. shortening or butter
- 2 eggs
- 2 T. milk
- 1 tsp. vanilla extract
- 3 ¼ c. flour
- 2 ½ tsp. baking powder
- ½ tsp. salt

Early in the day or the day before, in a large bowl, cream the shortening and the sugar. Add the eggs, extract and milk. In a medium bowl, mix the dry ingredients with a wire whisk. Add the dry ingredients to the large bowl. Mix with mixer until well combined. With hands, shape dough into a ball. Wrap with plastic wrap and refrigerate for 2 to 3 hours. Preheat oven to 400˚. Lightly grease cookie sheets. Roll half or ⅓ dough at a time and keep the rest refrigerated. For crisp cookies, roll dough paper thin. For softer cookies, roll ⅛ inch to ¼ inch thick.

# Dirt Dessert

20 oz. package Oreo cookies, crushed
8 oz. cream cheese
1 ½ sticks butter
1 c. powdered sugar
2 small packages instant chocolate pudding
9 oz. Cool Whip or whipped cream
1 package gummy worms

Crush Oreos and set aside. Mix cream cheese, butter and sugar together. Add to the mixture the instant pudding and then fold in the whipped cream.
To assemble, begin with a layer of the crushed Oreos on the bottom of an 8 inch flower pot. Top with a layer of the pudding mixture. Continue layering as described. Finish with a thick layer of Oreos on top to resemble dirt. Add gummy worms if desired. Serve it up with a garden trowel.

*Tip: Serve in an 8 inch flower pot.*

*** *Dirt Dessert is a great treat for children and especially fun to serve at school parties. This is a dessert a young child can make with their family and have a great time creating it together.*

# New Hampshire:
## Governor John Lynch and First Lady Susan Lynch

*Levi Hutchins of Concord invented the first alarm clock in 1787.*
*New Hampshire's State House is the oldest state capitol in which a legislature still meets in its original chambers.*

# Apple Pie

*Although New Hampshire does have an official Governor's Residence, it is rarely used by the Lynch family and does not have staff available for meal preparations. However, this apple pie has been made in the Lynch family for years and is a traditional New England dessert that everyone enjoys!*

Crust:
2 ½ c. all-purpose flour
1 tsp. salt
2 tsp. sugar
1-2 tsp. cinnamon or nutmeg or one tsp. of each
1 stick unsalted butter
6 T. vegetable shortening, chilled
6-8 T. ice water

**Filling:**

12 tart apples (Green Gravenstein or Granny Smith, etc.)
4 T. unsalted butter
½ c. and 2 T. sugar
2 T. cornstarch
¾ tsp. ground cinnamon
1 tsp. grated lemon zest
1 tsp. vanilla extract

Measure shortening and put into freezer to chill. Combine flour, salt, sugar and spice. Blend with a whisk. Add butter and shortening and work in with pastry blender until mixture resembles coarse crumbs. Sprinkle ice water over mixture, 2 tablespoons at a time and toss after each addition until you can gather dough into a ball. Transfer dough to floured surface and using the heel of your hand smear the dough away from you about ¼ cup at a time until all the dough has been smeared. Roll dough into a ball and divide it in half. Wrap each half in wax paper and refrigerate for 30 to 60 minutes. Roll half of the dough out on a floured surface to form an 11 inch circle and transfer to a 9 inch pie plate, pressing it to the bottom and the sides. Trim the dough leaving a 1 inch overhang.

Core, halve and peel apples and cut into 1 inch slices. Mix with melted butter in a large bowl. Add the remaining ingredients and mix until apples are evenly coated. Fill the bottom crust with apple mixture, mounding them high.

Place the top crust over the apples, tucking the edges underneath the bottom of the crust. Seal the edges of the crust together with a fork dipped in water. Brush the top of the piecrust with water and sprinkle with mixture of cinnamon and sugar. Cut vents in the piecrust top center. Bake at 350° for 1 ¼ hours or longer until the top is golden and the filling is bubbling. Place cookie sheet on the oven rack below to catch drippings.

# New Jersey:
## Governor Jon Corzine
## Given by: Mrs. William Hughes, Wife of New Jersey Representative

*Atlantic City has the longest boardwalk in the world and is where the street names came from for the game monopoly.*

*New Jersey has the most diners in the world.*

*The first Indian reservation was in New Jersey.*

## Shrimp and Pasta Salad

12 large cooked and deveined shrimp, cut into small pieces
½ c. chopped celery
½ c. chopped red bell pepper
¼ c. minced onion
½ medium sized mango, sliced into small pieces
Ground pepper to taste
Enough mayonnaise to moisten

Optional:
½ lb. capellini pasta
Oil to taste
½ c. Romano cheese

Salad Dressing:
1 packet Good Seasons Italian dressing
¼ c. wine vinegar
2 T. water
⅔ c. V8 juice

Mix all ingredients together and serve

chilled on a bed of lettuce. Serve with about a ½ pound of cooked and chilled capellini pasta, tossed with a little oil, Romano cheese and a no fat salad dressing.

Dressing: Mix vinegar and water. Add packet of Good Seasons. Mix until dissolved. Add V8 juice and mix again. Refrigerate until ready to use.

Yield: 4 servings

# New Mexico:
## Governor Bill Richardson and First Lady Barbara Richardson

*Each October, Albuquerque hosts the world's largest International Hot Air Balloon Fiesta.*

*The leaves of the Yucca, New Mexico's state flower, can be used to make rope, baskets and sandals.*

## New Mexican Flan

*This is one of First Lady Richardson's favorite desserts, served often at dinners for both friends and visiting dignitaries.*

**Red Chile Caramel:**
⅔ c. sugar
¼ c. water
2 tsp. ground red chile

**Custard:**
½ c. tequila
½ c. orange juice
½ c. sugar
5 whole eggs, lightly beaten
3 egg yolks, lightly beaten
¼ c. heavy cream
1 tsp. vanilla extract

Yield: 6 ½ cup molds

Preheat oven to 350˚. Cook caramel adding the red chile as the sugar turns golden brown, cook one more minute. Pour the caramel into 6 ½ cup molds coating the bottom and sides. Set aside.

Place tequila in shallow saucepan on low, being careful of high flames. Cook until flames subside. Pull from heat. Add fresh orange juice. When cool whisk in eggs, yolks, sugar and cream. Pour mixture into Red Chile Caramel coated molds.

Place molds in hot water bath reaching ½ way up the mold. Cover with parchment paper and foil. Bake for approximately 30 minutes. Center of flan should be lightly firm.

Take off cover and out of water bath. Let cool for 10 minutes. Place in refrigerator for at least 1 ½ hours before serving. Unmold flans onto individual plates making sure to pour caramel sauce on top.

# New York:
## Governor David A. Paterson and First Lady Michelle Paige Paterson

*Dairying is New York's most important farming activity with over 18,000 cattle and calf farms.*
*The Genesee River is one of the few rivers in the world that flows south to north.*
*In New York, they are blessed with the availability of local meats, dairy and vegetables.*

## Pork Loin with Apple Cornbread Stuffing, Cognac Reduction and Winter Squash Puree

*This recipe uses regional specialties, like the quark, that can be substituted with your local soft cheese. It is served as an ordinary dinner!*

¼ c. onion, diced small
¼ c. celery, diced small
¼ c. red pepper, diced small
¼ c. unsalted butter
1 tsp. salt
1 tsp. ground sage
¼ tsp. ground nutmeg
¼ tsp. ground black pepper
3 slices whole wheat bread
2 c. cornbread, cubed and crushed a bit
1 small Crispin apple, peeled, cored and small diced
¾ c. apple cider
4-5 oz. pork sausage, cooked and crumbled
1 (3-4 lb.) pork loin, butterflied butcher string
1 oz. clarified butter or olive oil

In a large sauté pan, sweat the onion, celery and red pepper over low heat until tender. Add the apple and cook another two minutes. In a large bowl, combine the onion/apple mixture with the remaining ingredients, except clarified butter or olive oil. Season with additional salt and pepper if desired. Line the middle of the pork loin with the stuffing and roll the ends together to seal in the stuffing. Tie the roast together with butcher string in 2-3 inch sections. Season the roast with salt, pepper and freshly chopped rosemary. Heat 1 ounce clarified butter or olive oil in a medium sauté pan. Sear the roast on all sides until golden brown. Transfer to a roasting pan and place in the oven. Roast in a 350˚ oven for 45 minutes to one hour, until an internal temperature reaches 120. Remove from oven. Reserve.

Cognac Sauce:
2 T. shallot, minced
1 T. garlic, minced
1 oz. brandy
½ oz. cider vinegar
1 c. veal stock
2 tsp. chopped rosemary
½ T. cold butter

In same pan used to brown the roast, add the shallots and garlic. Sauté until translucent, making sure to scrape all of the food left from the rendering of the pork. Deglaze the pan with the brandy and vinegar. Reduce by half. Add stock and reduce by ⅔. Adjust seasoning with salt and pepper. Add rosemary. Reserve.

**Winter Squash Puree:**
2 lb. winter squash (Hubbard, acorn, butternut, cheese pumpkin); peeled, seeded and sectioned
1 oz. unsalted butter
2 oz. maple syrup
$\frac{2}{3}$ c. quark (whole milk ricotta can be substituted)
Salt and pepper (to taste)

Cook the squash in salted boiling water until tender. Drain and press the sections through a potato ricer. Whisk the riced squash with the quark (or ricotta), butter and maple syrup. Season to taste. Slice the pork and serve it on a bed of squash puree.

# North Carolina:
## Governor Michael Easley and First Lady Mary Easley
### Given by: Chef Steve Moravick

*North Carolina is the largest producer of sweet potatoes in the nation. Students at a Wilson County school petitioned the North Carolina General Assembly for the establishment of the sweet potato as the official state vegetable.*

*Krispy Kreme Doughnut was founded in Winston-Salem.*

## Governor's Mansion Crab Cakes

¼ c. olive oil or more if necessary
¼ tsp. minced fresh garlic
¼ c. diced red onion
¼ c. diced celery
¼ c. diced red bell pepper
2 tsp. Dijon mustard
1 tsp. Old Bay Seasoning
1 tsp. Texas Pete Hot Sauce
1 tsp. Worcestershire Sauce
1 tsp. fresh lemon juice
1 tsp. fresh chopped tarragon
1 tsp. chopped capers
¼ tsp. dried dill
¼ tsp. black pepper
Pinch of kosher salt
1 large egg, lightly beaten
½ c. breadcrumbs, cracker meal, or Panko Japanese Bread-crumbs
Slightly less than ⅓ cup mayonnaise

1 lb. fresh lump crabmeat, picked over to remove cartilage
2 T. unsalted butter, or more if necessary

In a small skillet, cook the garlic, onion, celery and bell pepper in 1 T. olive oil over moderately low heat. Stir for 3 minutes or until they are softened. Transfer the mixture to a bowl and add the next 13 ingredients. Combine the mixture well. Add the crabmeat, stirring lightly until the mixture is just combined. Form the crab mixture into 12 cakes about ¾ inch thick. Dust a parchment paper lined sheet pan with more crumbs or meal, and place the crab cakes on the pan. Refrigerate for at least 1 hour.

In a large nonstick skillet, melt 1 T. of butter in 2 T. of olive oil over moderate heat. Fry the crab cakes in batches for about 3 minutes per side or until golden brown. (Add more butter or oil as necessary). Drain the crab cakes on paper towels. Serve immediately.

Yield: 6 servings

*Serving Suggestion: Appetizer, Salad or Entrée. Serve with mixed gourmet greens, Creole mustard dressing and corn relish. Enjoy!*

# Whole Roasted
# Veal Tenderloin

1 ½ - 2 lb. veal tenderloin,
trimmed of silver skin
3 T. Dijon mustard
1 tsp. minced garlic
½ tsp. fresh minced ginger
1 tsp. curry powder
½ tsp. coarse ground black
pepper
¼ tsp. kosher salt
1 tsp. Texas Pete
2 T. chopped fresh parsley
½ tsp. dried basil leaves
1 tsp. chopped fresh thyme
6-8 oz. extra-virgin olive oil
⅓ c. shelled pistachio nuts
toasted and ground fine
⅓ c. toasted pumpkin seeds
(pepitas) ground fine

Combine ingredients: mustard through thyme in a food processor fitted with a chopping blade. Start processor and slowly add the olive oil in a steady stream until an emulsion is formed. Mixture should be thick, similar to mayonnaise. Have a gallon sized Ziploc plastic bag ready. Coat trimmed tenderloin generously with the mustard mixture and place in plastic bag. Marinate in refrigerator 4 to 5 hours. Preheat convection oven to 350˚ or standard oven to 400˚.

Combine nuts and seeds and spread in the center of a piece of parchment paper. Take tenderloin from the bag and wipe some of the marinade off, but leave a thin coat so the nuts and seeds will adhere. Roll the tenderloin back and forth in the paper coating completely. Place tenderloin on a wire rack in a sheet pan. Be sure to tuck 1 inch to 2 inch of the tail underneath the loin to promote even roasting. Roast at 350˚ in a convection oven for 20 minutes. Remove, cover with foil and let rest to 10 minutes. Slice tenderloin into ½ inch bias cut slices. Serve with your favorite oven roasted vegetables and port wine demi-sauce.

Yield: 4 servings

# North Dakota:
## Governor John Hoeven and First Lady Mikey L. Hoeven

*North Dakota grows more sunflowers than any other state.*

*Turtle Lake celebrates turtles. Turtle Lake has erected a two-ton sculpture of a turtle near the entrance to the city. The town is the home of the annual United States Turtle Racing Championship.*

## Dakota Bread

1 package active dry yeast
½ c. warm water (105-110˚)
2 T. sunflower oil
1 egg
½ c. cottage cheese
¼ c. honey
1 tsp. salt
2 – 2 ½ c. bread flour
½ c. whole wheat flour
¼ c. wheat germ
¼ c. rye flour
¼ c. rolled oats
Cornmeal

Sprinkle yeast in warm water. Stir to dissolve. In a large bowl, mix sunflower oil, egg, cottage cheese, honey and salt. Add dissolved yeast and 2 cups bread flour, beating until flour is moistened. Gradually stir in whole wheat flour, wheat germ, rye flour and oats, plus enough bread flour to make a soft dough.

On a floured surface, knead dough about 10 minutes or until dough is smooth and elastic. Place dough in a greased bowl. Cover loosely with oiled plastic wrap and let rise until double in size, about 30 minutes.

Punch dough down. Shape into one round loaf. Place into a greased glass pie pan sprinkled with cornmeal. Cover with oiled plastic wrap and let rise until doubled in size (about 1 hour).

Brush with egg white and sprinkle with wheat germ, sunflower kernels or oatmeal. Bake at 350˚ for 35 to 40 minutes. If too dark, cover loosely with foil the last 10 to 15 minutes of baking. Remove from pie pan and cool on a wire rack.

Yield: 1-2 lb. loaf

# Balsamic Chicken Salad

8 boneless, skinless chicken breasts
1 green pepper – ¼ inch slices
1 red pepper – ¼ inch slices
1 yellow pepper – ¼ inch slices
4 small carrots
Broccoli florets – cut small
Greens of choice

Balsamic Vinaigrette Marinade:
1 oz. olive oil
1 oz. of honey
1 oz. Dijon mustard
1 oz. balsamic vinegar
½ tsp. minced garlic
Salt and pepper to taste

*Note: You will need to make 3 portions of the marinade.*

Marinate chicken breasts in balsamic vinaigrette overnight. Marinate vegetables in balsamic vinaigrette for at least one hour prior to grilling. Grill chicken breasts and vegetables. Allow to cool to room temperature and slice chicken breasts in ¼ inch slices. Place grilled vegetables on bed of greens. Fan sliced chicken breasts on greens/vegetables. Drizzle additional dressing just prior to serving.

Yield: 8 servings

# Ohio:
## Governor Ted Strickland and First Lady Frances Strickland Given by: Mrs. Doug Applegate, Wife of Ohio Representative

*Cleveland boasts America's first traffic light. It began on Aug. 5, 1914.*
*"Hang On Sloopy" is the official state rock song.*

## Escalloped Oysters

1 pt. oysters
1 c. cracker crumbs, medium coarse
½ c. butter, melted or oleo
½ tsp. salt
Dash of pepper
¾ c. cream
¼ c. oyster liquid
¼ tsp. Worcestershire sauce

Drain oysters and save liquid. Combine crumbs, butter, salt and pepper. Spread ⅓ of crumbs in greased 8 inch square pan or baking dish. Cover with ½ of the oysters. Using another ⅓ crumbs, spread a second layer. Cover with remaining oysters. Combine cream, oyster liquid and sauce. Pour over oysters. Top with last of crumbs. Bake at 350° for 40 minutes.

Yield: 8 servings

# Oklahoma:
## Governor Brad Henry and First Lady Kimberly Henry Given by: Executive Chef David McAlvain

*There is an operating oil well on state capitol grounds called Capitol Site No. 1. Oklahoma is one of only two states whose capital city's name includes the state name. The other is Indianapolis, Indiana. Oklahoma has more man-made lakes than any other state, with over one million surface acres of water.*

## Mustard Crusted Catfish

4 (8 oz.) catfish fillets
2 (5 ¼ oz.) jars of Creole mustard
¼ c. white wine
1 tsp. salt
1 tsp. cracked black pepper
Peanut oil for frying
1 ½ c. yellow cornmeal
1 c. flour
½ c. corn starch
2 T. of Creole seasoning

Combine mustard, wine, salt and pepper and then pour over the catfish. Marinate for 1 ½ hours. Mix all dry ingredients together. Remove catfish from marinade and coat catfish with dry ingredients. Fry in peanut oil, three minutes per side. Enjoy!

Yield: 4 servings

## Rosemary Mustard Crusted Rack of Lamb

3 eight bone rack of lamb, Frenched
¾ c. fresh rosemary, chopped
4 (5 ¼ oz.) Creole mustard
cracked black pepper and salt (to taste)
2 c. of Japanese bread crumbs
4 T. olive oil

Heat oven to 400˚ and heat oil in a skillet. Sear the lamb on all sides and set it aside. Mix together rosemary and mustard. Coat each rack with mustard and rosemary. Cover bones of each rack with aluminum foil and place in pan with a rack. Cover each mustard coated rack with bread crumbs. Spray each rack with pan coating. Bake in a 400˚ oven for 30 minutes or until instant-read thermometer reads 120 – 125˚ then remove racks from oven. Let rest for 10 to 15 minutes before slicing.

Yield: 3 servings

# Oregon:
## Governor Ted Kulongoski and First Lady Mary Oberst

*Oregon's state flag pictures a beaver on its reverse side. It is the only state flag to carry two separate designs.*
*The hazelnut is Oregon's official state nut. The hazelnut is also known as the filbert.*

## Oregon Strawberry Salad

2 bunches of organically grown spinach (washed, stems removed)
2 pt. of Oregon strawberries, each berry halved

Dressing:
⅓ c. sugar
2 T. sesame seeds
1 ½ tsp. onion, minced
¼ tsp. Worcestershire sauce
¼ tsp. paprika
½ c. oil
¼ c. cider vinegar

Mix ingredients for dressing. Spoon over salad and toss!

# Pennsylvania:
## Governor Edward Rendell and First Lady Marjorie Rendell

*Hershey, Pennsylvania is considered the Chocolate Capital of the United States. Philadelphia is home to the cheesesteak sandwich, water ice, soft pretzels and TastyKakes.*

*During the depression, canned goods served as admission to The Star Theater in Mercersburg to help supply the local soup kitchen.*

## "Swedish Dream" Cookies

*The baking of these family favorites are part of First Lady Rendell's childhood memories, a tradition which she has proudly kept alive. The first lady has such wonderful recollections of baking these melt-in-your-mouth delights with her mother and sister in their Wilmington, Delaware home. Additionally, these shortbread cookies have now become a holiday favorite in the Pennsylvania Governor's Residence where the first lady fondly bakes the much-loved cookies to share with staff, family and friends during the holiday season!*

> 1 c. (2 sticks) butter at room temperature
> 1 c. sugar
> ½ tsp. vanilla
> 1 ½ c. sifted flour
> ½ tsp. baking powder
> Walnuts

Cream butter at high speed of electric mixer until very light and fluffy. With mixer at low speed, add sugar in a stream. Increase speed to medium and mix until very fluffy. Add vanilla and mix. Stir baking powder into flour. With mixer at low speed, slowly add dry ingredients to butter/sugar mixture, a tablespoon or 2 at a time. Increase speed to medium and beat to fully incorporate dry ingredients.

Drop by teaspoon onto lightly greased cookie sheet.

Wrap the bottom of a small glass in a damp kitchen towel, not terry cloth. "Bop" each piece of dough with the glass to flatten. If towel begins to stick to the dough, move the glass to a clean place. Press a piece of walnut into the center of each cookie and sprinkle with sugar. Bake at 325° until the edges begin to turn golden, about 8 to 10 minutes. Don't over bake.

# Rhode Island:
## Governor Don Carcieri and First Lady Suzanne Carcieri

*Judge Darius Baker imposed the first jail sentence for speeding in an automobile on August 28, 1904, in Newport. The first circus in the United States was in Newport in 1774.*

## Spaghetti and Meatballs

*Spaghetti and Meatballs is a favorite of Governor Carcieri and the whole Carcieri family. We have served this for many family meals and it is enjoyed by all of our children and grandchildren.*

Meatballs:
2 lbs. ground beef
1 c. bread crumbs
3 eggs
2 T. garlic powder (to taste)
1 T. oregano
Salt and pepper (to taste)

Combine ingredients in large bowl. Use hands to form into balls.

Sauce:
2 -3 large onions
Olive oil
3 large cans of tomato puree
1 – 2 T. of garlic powder
1 – 2 T. of salt and pepper
2 T. oregano

Cut large onions. Sauté them in a very large pan in olive oil until browned lightly. Pour in three large cans of tomato puree. Add garlic powder, oregano, salt and pepper. Stir and add the formed balls into the sauce. Cook slowly over low heat for four hours.

# South Carolina:
## Governor Mark Sanford and First Lady Jenny Sanford Given by: Executive Chef Andy Marchant CEC, South Carolina's Governor's Mansion

*The walls of the American fort on Sullivan Island, in Charleston Harbor, were made of spongy palmetto logs. This was helpful in protecting the fort because the British cannonballs bounced off the logs.*
*The state dance of South Carolina is the Shag!*

## Carolina Crab Cakes

*Each spring, the spouses of House and Senate members, past and present, meet at the South Carolina Governor's Mansion for a luncheon. This meal was served at last year's lunch.*

   1 lb. fresh lump crabmeat, drained
   1 egg beaten
   ¼ c. Panko breadcrumbs
   ¼ tsp. Old Bay seasoning
   1 tsp. red pepper, diced very fine
   1 tsp. red onion, diced very fine
   1 tsp. mayonnaise
   1 T. butter for sautéing
   ¼ tsp. white truffle oil
   Salt and pepper (to taste)

Mix all ingredients well in a medium bowl. Mold into four 4 ounce cakes. Dust cakes in flour and sauté in a large skillet with 1 tablespoon of butter until golden brown on both sides.

## Sweet Hominy Succotash

   2 T. olive oil
   4 oz. country ham or pancetta
   ¼ c. fennel or anise, diced
   ¼ carrot, peeled and diced
   ½ c. onion, diced
   ¼ c. red bell pepper, diced
   Pinch crushed red pepper
   1 bay leaf
   1 lb. frozen baby lima beans
   Chicken stock as needed
   Salt and pepper to taste
   1 c. white hominy, drained and rinsed
   ¾ c. heavy cream
   1 T. fresh thyme
   1 T. fresh parsley

Heat oil and render pancetta crisp. Add diced vegetables and caramelize. Add crushed red pepper and bay leaf. Add baby lima's. Add enough stock to just cover and simmer till tender. Combine hominy and cream in a sauce pan and cook until thickened slightly. Add to vegetable mixture. At service, add thyme and parsley and heat thoroughly.

# South Dakota:
## Governor Mike Rounds and First Lady Jean Rounds

*Clark is the "Potato Capital of South Dakota," as well as home to the world famous Mashed Potato Wrestling contest.*

## Prime Rib Rub

*South Dakota certified Beef Prime Rib is served often at the South Dakota's Governor's Residence.*

> ½ c. kosher salt
> 3 T. dry mustard
> 2 T. coarse black pepper
> 4 tsp. garlic powder
> 4 tsp. onion powder
> 4 tsp. celery seed
> 4 tsp. oregano leaves
> 4 tsp. dried thyme
> 4 tsp. ground coriander

Blend all ingredients. Rub prime rib with olive oil. Season rib very well with ingredients. Cook fat side up at 325° for 3 to 4 hours or until a meat thermometer registers 140 – 145°.

# Tennessee:
## Governor Phil Bredesen and First Lady Andrea Conte
## Given by: Chef Hilda Pope, Manager of the Tennessee Executive Residence

*Nashville's Grand Ole Opry is the longest continuously running live radio program in the world. Since 1925, it has had a broadcast every Friday and Saturday night.*

*Coca-Cola was first bottled in 1899 at a plant on Patten Parkway in downtown Chattanooga after two local attorneys purchased the bottling rights to the drink for $1.00.*

## Poached Salmon with Lemon Mayonnaise

Salmon:
¾ c. dry white wine sauce
4 whole peppercorns
4 (6 oz.) salmon filets, skinned

Mayonnaise:
1 c. mayonnaise
2 T. fresh lemon juice
2 tsp. grated lemon peel
2 T. chopped fresh chives
2 T. chopped fresh dill

To serve:
Bibb or Butter lettuce leaves
4 lemon slices
8 lemon wedges

For salmon:
Combine first 3 ingredients in a deep skillet. Bring to a boil before adding the salmon. Cover and simmer until just cooked through, about 9 minutes per an inch of thickness. Cool salmon in poaching liquid. Remove from liquid, drain on paper towels, cover and chill until cold.

For Mayonnaise:
Combine mayonnaise, lemon juice, lemon peel, chives and dill in a bowl. Season to taste with salt and fresh pepper. Cover and chill.

To serve:
Line plates with lettuce. Top with salmon. Make cut in each lemon slice from center to edge. Twist lemon slices and place atop salmon. Garnish with lemon wedges and tomatoes. Serve with mayonnaise. (Hint: Pipe mayonnaise with a pastry tip.)

Yield: 4 servings

# Rice Salad with Arugula, Pine Nuts and Olives

3 c. chicken stock
2 c. long-grain rice (Uncle Ben's holds its shape best)
5 T. olive oil
¾ c. slivered, pitted olives such as Calamata
2 T. fresh lemon juice
1 ½ oz. package fresh arugula, stemmed and chopped
3 green onions, chopped small
½ c. pine nuts or more, toasted
⅓ c. freshly grated Romano cheese
2 T. capers
2 T. fresh chopped basil
2 – 3 T. roasted red peppers, cut into strips
Salt and fresh pepper to taste
Optional: quartered hard cooked eggs

Bring 3 cups chicken stock to boil in heavy medium saucepan. Add rice. Bring to boil, reduce heat to low, cover and cook until chicken broth is absorbed, about 20 minutes. Turn heat off and let stand 5 minutes.
Fluff rice with fork and transfer to large bowl. Mix in 5 tablespoons olive oil. Then add all remaining ingredients. Season salad liberally with pepper. If dry, can add a ¼ cup mayonnaise. Do not refrigerate, best warm or room temperature.

Yield: 8 servings

# Dilled Cucumber Salad

¼ c. sour cream
2 T. mayonnaise
2 T. minced fresh dill
2 English cucumbers
1 – 2 tsp. sugar
2 T. seasoned rice vinegar
Salt and pepper to taste

Cut the English cucumber lengthwise. Seed and slice crosswise into ⅛ inch thick pieces. Salt with ½ teaspoon salt and let sit for 30 minutes. Rinse with cold water and drain in a colander.
In a bowl, whisk together the sour cream, mayonnaise, lime juice and dill. Salt and pepper to taste. Stir cucumbers into dressing. Make sure you drain the salad before serving, it gives off quite a bit of liquid.

Yield: 6 servings

# *Texas:*
## Governor Rick Perry and First Lady Anita Perry

*Dr Pepper was invented in Waco in 1885. The Dublin Dr Pepper, 85 miles west of Waco, still uses pure imperial cane sugar in its product. There is no period after the Dr in Dr Pepper.*

## Chicken Piccata

4 boneless, skinless chicken breasts
½ c. flour
4 T. olive oil
1 shallot minced
1 c. chicken broth or stock
2 lemons- 1 juiced and 1 cut into half moon slices
2 T. rinsed capers
2 T. butter
2 T. fresh parsley leaves, chopped

Heat oven to 250˚. Pound each chicken breast between 2 pieces of plastic wrap until ¼ inch thick. Season each cutlet with salt, pepper and coat each cutlet with flour. Heat oil in heavy bottomed skillet and cook each cutlet 3 minutes on each side. Transfer to baking sheet and place in oven. Sauté shallot in now empty skillet for 1 minute. Add chicken stock and scrape browned bits from bottom of skillet. Simmer about 4 minutes. Add juice of one lemon and the capers. Cook for one minute. Add lemon slices and butter. Serve chicken cutlets with sauce, sprinkle with parsley. Enjoy!

*Yield: 4 servings*

*The remarkable Sarah Bishop has made hundreds of gallons of this delicious summer tea for receptions and events at the Governor's Mansion. It is incredibly popular and the recipe, though somewhat complicated, is well worth the effort. The torch has been passed to Dean Peterson who now makes the punch for various Governor's Mansion events.*

## Summer Peach Tea Punch

3 family size tea bags
4 c. fresh mint
4 c. water
12-oz. can lemonade concentrate
2 bottles Knudsen's Peach Nectar® (Do not substitute: Purchase at whole food markets or other food health stores.)
2 liters ginger ale
2 liters soda
½ to 1 c. simple syrup (Simple syrup: 2 parts sugar to 1 part water. Bring to a slow boil until clear- about 4 minutes.)

Boil water to steep tea and mint. Steep about 15 minutes. Remove tea bags. Leave mint in solution until cool. Strain into 2 gallon containers. Add lemonade, peach nectar and syrup concentrate. Add 2 liters ginger ale and 2 liters soda. Taste before adding simple syrup.

Yield: 2 gallons

# Utah:
## Governor Jon Huntsman and First Lady Mary Kaye Huntsman

*Salt Lake City was originally named Great Salt Lake City. Great was dropped from the name in 1868. Average snowfall in the mountains near Salt Lake City is 500 inches. Utah has 11,000 miles of fishing streams and 147,000 acres of lakes and reservoirs.*

## Summer Salad

Dressing:
12 T. olive oil
6 T. balsamic vinegar
2 tsp. spicy honey mustard
½ T. of fresh chopped parsley

Salad:
2 bags of mixed greens
1 container of crumbled blue cheese
1 c. red grapes, halved
1 – 2 pears, cubed
½ c. dried cranberries
½ c. pistachios

Combine dressing ingredients and whisk until creamy. Place salad items in a large bowl and toss. Add dressing to taste.

# Vermont:
## Governor Jim Douglas and First Lady Dorothy Douglas

*Montpelier, Vermont is the only U.S. State Capital without a McDonalds.*
*Ben & Jerry's Ice Cream company gives their ice cream waste to the local Vermont farmers who use it to feed their hogs. The hogs seem to like all of the flavors except Mint Oreo.*

## Maple Walnut Squares

*We are one of six states without an official Governor's Residence, so we eat these at home!*

1 ½ c. flour
¼ c. brown sugar
½ c. butter
⅔ c. brown sugar
1 c. maple syrup
2 eggs
½ tsp. vanilla
2 T. flour
¼ tsp. salt
1 c. chopped walnuts

Combine 1 ½ cups flour and ¼ cup brown sugar. Cut in butter until crumbly. Press into 9x13 pan and bake at 350˚ for 15 minutes.
Combine ⅔ cup brown sugar and syrup in saucepan, simmer for 5 minutes. Pour over slightly beaten eggs, stirring constantly with whisk. Stir in vanilla, 2 tablespoons flour and salt. Pour over baked crust, sprinkle walnuts on top. Bake 350˚ for 20 minutes.

# Virgin Islands:
## Governor John deJongh, Jr. and First Lady Cecile deJongh

*During the 17th century the Virgin Islands were divided between the English and the Danish colonies. The Danish Islands were purchased by the United States in 1917. Since this time, they have been transformed into a popular tourist destination. The port of Charlotte Amalie on St. Thomas is a popular site for cruise ships.*

## Kallaloo Recipe

1 gal. water
2 lb. of spinach
1 lb. of okra
½ c. of chopped celery
1 c. of chopped onions
3 cloves garlic, minced
1 tsp. ground cumin
¾ tsp. of ground all spice
½ tsp. of hot pepper
¼ tsp. of salt
½ tsp. of thyme leaves
½ c. of onion
½ tsp. of black pepper
½ c. of green pepper
½ c. of red pepper
1 c. of fresh parsley
2 lb. baked or grill fish
½ lb. crab
½ lb. shrimp
½ tsp. adobo
2 c. milk
½ tsp. basil leaves

Boil spinach and okra for 15 to 20 minutes. Put all your seasonings in and let boil for 10 to 15 minutes. Then put in your milk and let boil for 2 minutes. Add your fish, shrimp and crab and let it simmer down.

# Virginia:
## Governor Tim Kaine and First Lady Anne Holton
Given by: Jason Babson, Mansion Chef

*Virginia was named for England's "Virgin Queen," Elizabeth I.*
*The Pentagon building in Arlington is the largest office building in the world.*

## Asian Lo Mein Salad

One box of Lo Mein noodles or spaghetti cooked and cooled
3 red peppers, julienned
1 bunch green onions
1 red onion, julienned
3 bunches broccoli, chopped
½ lb. snow peas
4 carrots sliced thin
1 container crimini mushrooms sliced
½ lb. green beans (blanched) cut into ½ inch pieces
1 bunch asparagus (blanched) cut into ½ inch pieces
½ bunch cilantro, chopped

Asian sauce:
½ c. soy sauce
4 T. garlic chili sauce
1 T. fish sauce
4 T. honey
2 T. sherry wine vinegar
2 T. rice wine vinegar
2 T. sesame seeds
¼ c. sesame oil
1 tsp. lemongrass extract

*(The chili sauce and lemongrass can be found in any Asian food store. The lemongrass is optional.)*
Mix all ingredients in a bowl with a wire whisk. If dressing is too strong, add 1 tablespoon honey to cut the strength. Add dressing to vegetables and pasta. Toss and let sit at least one hour before serving. Remember to toss just before serving because dressing will be on bottom of bowl. You may add more vegetables or reduce amount of pasta to satisfy your taste.

# Washington:
## Governor Chris Gregoire and First Gentleman Mike Gregoire
Given by: Chef Kyle Fulwiler, Executive Mansion

*The state of Washington is the only state to be named after a United States president. Washington state produces more apples than any other state in the union. Washington state has more glaciers than the other 47 contiguous states combined.*

## Crab Cakes

    1 lb. crabmeat
    ¼ c. mayonnaise
    1 tsp. chopped parsley
    1 stalk celery, chopped fine
    3 shallots, chopped fine
    ¼ tsp. Tabasco
    ½ c. dried bread crumbs
    2 eggs beaten slightly
    2 c. Panko
    ½ c. pommery mustard
    3 T. mayonnaise
    ½ c. butter, clarified

Flake the crabmeat apart in a large bowl with two forks. Add the mayonnaise, parsley, celery, shallots and Tabasco. Stir with a spatula until all ingredients are evenly mixed. Mix in the dried bread crumbs. Mix well. Mix the eggs into the mixture.

Place the Panko in a pie plate or other flat, low-sided dish. Scoop out heaping tablespoons of the crab mixture on to the Panko, forming cakes that are two inches in diameter and about 3/8 inch thick. Flip each to coat the other side. Place them on a baking sheet. Chill the cakes for 30 minutes. Mix the mustard and mayonnaise in a serving dish or into individual condiment cups. Cover and chill.

# West Virginia:
## Governor Joe Manchin, III and First Lady Gayle Manchin

*West Virginia is considered the southern most northern state and the northern most southern state.*
*West Virginia has the oldest population of any state. The median age is 40. Nearly 70% of West Virginia is covered by forests.*

## Lemon Sorbet

    8 large lemons
    2 inch piece of fresh ginger
    2 c. water
    1 ½ c. Splenda
    Ice
    3 lemon zest

Combine Splenda, water and ginger in a pan and heat until hot. Let cool, then combine in blender with one cup of juice from lemons and blend for one minute. Add lemon zest from 3 lemons and ice to fill blender. Blend until ice is totally crushed. Then put in ice cream or sorbet maker or put in freezer stirring every once in awhile until desired consistency. This is one of the ways we serve refreshing and delightful desserts that are healthy.

# Wisconsin:
## Governor Jim Doyle and First Lady Jessica Doyle

*Wisconsin produces more milk than any other state.*
*Two Rivers is the home of the ice cream sundae.*

## Door County Sweet Cherry Crisp

*This is a favorite summer treat at the Executive Residence. The Cabinet of Governor Jim Doyle often enjoys the Door County Sweet Cherry Crisp filled with flavors of Wisconsin.*

> 2 c. packed brown sugar
> 2 c. old-fashioned rolled oats
> 3 ⅔ c. flour, divided
> 1 ½ c. (3 sticks) Wisconsin butter, room temperature
> 4 c. thawed and drained frozen, sweetened Door County cherries
> Whipped cream or vanilla ice cream

Preheat oven to 350°. In a large bowl, combine brown sugar, oats and 3 cups flour. Cut in butter with fingers or two knives. Place half the mixture in greased 10 x 8 inch glass pan, pressing it down lightly. If desired, a metal pan can be used, but the crisp will not look as attractive when served.
In medium bowl, combine cherries and remaining ⅔ cup flour. Spoon evenly. Add remaining ⅔ cup flour and spoon evenly over mixture in pan. Evenly sprinkle remaining crumb mixture over berry layer.

Bake in preheated oven for 50 minutes or until bubbly and dark brown. Serve warm with ice cream or cold with whipped cream.
Variation: Add 1 cup crushed pecans to crumb mixture.

Yield: 8 servings

# Wyoming:
## Governor Dave Freudenthal and First Lady Nancy Freudenthal
### Given by: Becky Brown, Executive Chef

*Wyoming was the first state to give women the right to vote.*

*The Wind River actually changes its name in the middle of the stream becoming the Big Horn River at a site at the north end of the Wind River Canyon, where each year the Native Americans hold a ceremony depicting the "Wedding of the Waters."*

## Flank Steak Roulade

*This is an original recipe from the Freudenthal's Executive Chef, Becky Brown. It has been served for family dinners as well as when entertaining a former ambassador.*

1 - 1 ½  lb. flank steak, pound evenly
1 ¾ c. pesto
2-3 slices prosciutto
3-4 slices provolone

Spread pesto over flank steak. Cover with provolone and prosciutto. Roll flank in the opposite direction of the length of the fibers. Tie roll with kitchen string. Brown all sides in skillet. Roast at 350° for 20 to 30 minutes until desired doneness.

Slice and serve with Pesto Sauce.

Pesto Sauce:
1 c. pesto
5 c. cream

Warm slightly. Enjoy!

# First Ladies
## of America

# Notes

# First Ladies of America

No first lady of a state or a nation plans to ever be a first lady of a state or a nation. When our partner becomes a governor or president, as spouses we still hold on to our lives before we began this new journey. One day we will return to that life. These presidents' wives gave us great family recipes from our earliest days of American history. I'm sure most of their recipes were served when their dinner bell rang at **The White House**.

## First Lady
## Martha Washington

## Chess Cakes

    1 c. butter
    1 c. sugar
    6 egg yolks, beaten
    ⅓ c. dry white wine
    1 T. lemon juice
    Grated rind of 1 lemon
    ¼ tsp. salt
    Pastry for 1 (9 inch) pie or 12
    tarts (made in muffin tins or
    fluted patty pan)

Cream butter and beat in ½ cup sugar, slowly, reserving the rest of the sugar. Beat egg yolks with salt until light and lemon colored. Slowly beat in the remaining ½ cup sugar. With a whisk, fold in the lemon juice and grated lemon rind. Combine with the creamed mixture, stirring in the wine. Pour into pie shells or tart shells. Bake at 350° for 50 to 60 minutes until set.

# First Lady
# Abigail Adams

## Baked Salmon

Salmon
Skinned eel
1 pt. oysters
2 T. oyster liquid, reserved
4 c. bread crumbs
3 T. butter, melted
3 eggs, beaten whole
1 T. parsley, chopped
1 tsp. thyme
Dash of pepper
Salt
Dash of cloves
Dash of nutmeg
Pt. of claret

Sauce:
Drippings from the salmon
Some shrimp
Pickled mushrooms
2 anchovies

Clean the salmon. Wash and dry it. Lard it with a skinned eel. Combine the oysters (reserve liquid), bread crumbs, melted butter, eggs, chopped parsley, thyme, salt, pepper, cloves, nutmeg and 1 tablespoon oyster liquid. Fill the salmon with stuffing. Baste well with butter. Lay salmon on a rack in a roasting pan. Pour a pint of claret over it and cover salmon with buttered paper. Bake in a preheated oven (550°) for 10 minutes. Reduce the heat to 425°. Bake 20 to 35 minutes longer. Allow 10 minutes per pound for the first 4 pounds and 5 minutes for each additional pound. Baste several times.

Ten minutes before the baking is done, uncover and bake until done. Boil ingredients together for sauce.

# First Lady
# Rachel Jackson

## Strawberry Mousse

2 pt. strawberries, hulled, sliced
¾ c. sugar
2 envelopes unflavored gelatin
½ c. water
1 tsp. almond extract
1 c. whipping cream
¼ c. rum

Mash 2 cups of the strawberries until smooth. Mix ½ cup of the sugar and the gelatin in a small saucepan. Stir in water. Let stand 1 minute. Heat, stirring constantly over low heat until gelatin dissolves.

Add gelatin mixture and almond extract to strawberry puree and mix well. Refrigerate covered, until mixture mounds slightly when dropped from spoon, about one hour.

Beat cream in small mixing bowl until stiff and fold into gelatin mixture. Pour into 1 quart mold. Refrigerate covered until firm, about three hours. Mix remaining strawberries, remaining ¼ cup of sugar and rum in medium bowl. Let stand one hour. Blend 1 cup strawberries and rum until smooth. Mix with remaining strawberries and rum. To serve, dip mold into hot water. Invert and unmold onto serving dish. Serve with strawberry and rum sauce.

Yield: 8 servings

# First Lady
# Jacqueline Kennedy

## Fish Chowder

2 lbs. haddock
2 oz. salt pork, diced
2 onions, sliced
4 large potatoes, diced
1 c. celery, chopped
I bay leaf, crumbled
1 qt. milk
2 T. butter
1 tsp. salt
Freshly ground pepper

Simmer haddock in 2 cups water for 15 minutes. Drain. Reserve broth. Remove bones from fish. Sauté diced pork until crisp. Remove and set aside. Sauté onions in pork fat until golden brown. Add fish, potatoes, celery, bay leaf, salt and pepper. Pour in fish broth. Add enough boiling water to make 3 cups liquid. Simmer for 30 minutes. Add milk and butter and simmer for five minutes. Serve chowder sprinkled with diced pork.

Yield: 6 servings

# First Lady
# Claudia "Lady Bird" Johnson

## Tortilla Soup Giraud

1 ½ onions, chopped
1 bell pepper, chopped
2 potatoes, diced
2 carrots, diced
¼ c. celery, diced
3 ½ qt. chicken stock
¾ c. garbanzo beans
1 lb. chicken meat, diced
2 T. chili powder
1 T. comino
1 tsp. pepper
1 tsp. granulated garlic
2 T. cilantro, chopped

Garnish:
Fried tortilla strips
Lime
Avacado

Sauté onion and bell pepper for ten seconds. Add carrots, celery and potatoes. Sauté two more minutes. Add hot chicken stock and simmer five to ten minutes. Add seasonings. Finish by adding chicken meat and cilantro. Slow simmering improves flavor. Garnish and serve. (Strips of avocado and lime juice are very important.)

# First Lady
## Patricia Ryan Nixon

## Ham Mousse

½ c. cooked ham, finely ground
1 c. tomato juice
1 c. beef consommé
½ tsp. paprika
4 T. cold water
1 envelope gelatin
2 c. cream, whipped
Salt to taste
Mayonnaise
Few drops of lemon juice
A little heavy cream
Finely chopped chives

Mix first four ingredients and bring to a boil. Dissolve gelatin in water. Add to ham mixture. Put in refrigerator to cool, stirring occasionally. When it begins to slightly congeal, fold in the whipped cream. Add salt to taste. Pour into one large mold or smaller individual molds. Let set in refrigerator until firm. Unmold and garnish with watercress. Serve with mayonnaise thinned with a few drops of lemon juice and a little heavy cream, adding finely chopped chives.

Yield: 4-6 servings

# First Lady
## Betty B. Ford

## Carrot Vichyssoise

2 c. potatoes, diced and peeled
1 ¼ c. carrots, sliced and peeled
1 T. onion, chopped
3 c. canned chicken broth
White pepper and salt to taste
1 c. sour cream
Chopped chives and parsley

Simmer potatoes and carrots in chicken broth with the onion until tender. Season to taste. Cool puree in a blender and chill thoroughly in refrigerator. Approximately 1 hour before serving, fold in 1 cup of sour cream to which has been added 1 heaping teaspoon chopped chives. Serve with a topping of chopped parsley.

Yield: 6 servings

# First Lady
## Rosalynn Carter

## "Plains Special" Cheese Ring

1 lb. grated sharp Cheddar cheese
1 c. mayonnaise
1 c. nuts, chopped
1 small onion, grated
1 jar strawberry preserves
Black pepper to taste
Dash of cayenne

Mix and mold with hands into desired shape. (We mold into a ring.) Refrigerate until chilled. To serve, fill center with strawberry preserves. Can be served as a compliment to a main meal or as an hors d' oeuvre with crackers.

# First Lady
# Nancy Reagan

## Monkey Bread

¾ oz. yeast or 1 package dry yeast
1 to 1 ¼ c. milk
3 eggs
3 T. sugar
1 tsp. salt
3 ½ c. flour
6 oz. butter, room temperature
½ lb. butter, melted
2 (9 inch) ring molds

In a bowl, mix yeast with part of milk until dissolved. Add 2 eggs and beat. Mix in dry ingredients. Add remaining milk, a little bit at a time, mixing thoroughly. Cut in butter until blended. Knead dough. Let rise 1 to 1 ½ hours until double in size. Knead again. Let rise 40 minutes. Roll dough onto flour board. Shape into a log. Cut log into 28 pieces of equal size. Shape each piece of dough into a ball. Roll in melted butter. Use half of the pieces in each buttered and floured molds. Place seven balls in each mold, leaving spaces in between. Place remaining balls on top. Spacing evenly. Let dough rise in mold. Brush tops with remaining egg. Bake in preheated oven at 375˚ until golden brown, approximately 15 minutes.

# First Lady
# Barbara Bush

## Barbequed Chicken

Marinade:
1 3-lb. fryer, quartered
1 large garlic clove, crushed
1 tsp. salt
½ tsp. freshly ground pepper
1 T. oil
3 T. lemon juice

Put ingredients in a heavy Ziploc bag. Shake, to coat well. Refrigerate for 24 hours if possible, turning the bag several times. When coals are ready, place chicken on the grill, skin side up. Baste with the marinade. Cook until well browned before turning. (If baking on oven, bake at 400˚, skin side down first.) About 20 minutes before chicken is done, begin using your favorite bottled barbeque sauce or the homemade version which follows.

Barbeque Sauce:
¼ c. cider vinegar
2 ¼ c. water
¾ c. sugar
1 stick butter or margarine
⅓ c. yellow mustard
2 onions, coarsely chopped
½ tsp. each salt and pepper

Bring to a boil. Cook on low 20 minutes or until onion is tender.

Then add:
½ c. Worcestershire
2 ½ c. catsup
6-8 T. lemon juice
Cayenne pepper to taste.

Simmer slowly for 45 minutes. Taste for seasoning. This sauce freezes well.

Yield: 4 servings

# First Lady
# Hillary Clinton

## Sweet and Sour Slaw

3 lbs. cabbage, grated
1 onion, chopped
1 green pepper, chopped
1 carrot, grated
1 c. sugar
¾ c. oil
¾ c. vinegar
1 ½ tsp. salt
1 tsp. celery seed
1 tsp. dry mustard

Combine cabbage, onion and green pepper. Pour sugar over vegetables. In saucepan, combine oil, vinegar, salt, celery seed and mustard. Heat to boiling. Pour over slaw and stir. Refrigerate overnight.

# First Lady
# Laura Bush

## Carrot-Ginger Soup

3 T. olive oil
1 onion, peeled and chopped
1 celery stalk, chopped
10 carrots, peeled and chopped into 1 inch pieces
¼ cup ginger, peeled and finely diced
Salt (to taste)
6 c. water
4 T. sugar
2 T. rice wine vinegar
Cilantro leaves

In a medium stock pot, sauté onions and carrots in olive oil for 4 minutes or until onions are translucent. Add ginger, water and sugar and let simmer for 25 minutes until carrots are soft. Let cool. In a lender or food processor, puree until smooth. Season with rice wine vinegar and salt to taste. Serve hot or chilled with cilantro leaves to garnish.

# Notes

# End Note

As I came to the close of this book, I began to look for a wonderful way to end this project that I've enjoyed working on for quite sometime. The day before turning it over to Sherrie Stanyard, my dear friend Julia Butts handed me this beautiful song about our beloved Alabama. It was discovered in a piano bench by a friend.

After reading Mr. Z. T. Spencer's words, I passionately agree, as many of you will join me in saying "I love you, Alabama."

**From the sheet music cover:**

The author, after residing in Alabama for 15 years, sought a more fair and favored section; but after a residence of four years in Florida, three years in Texas, and fifteen years in California, he returned to his first love – Alabama, where he received so true and hearty a welcome that he was prompted to give expression to his feelings by writing this beautiful song, 'I Love You, Alabama.'

# I Love You, Alabama

I love you, Alabama, you're the grandest of the states;
I love your lofty mountains, your rivers and your lakes;
I love your hills and valleys, your summer, fall and spring;
I love your fields and forests and the birds that in them sing,
I love you for your waterfalls, your seashore and your plains,
Your hills of coal and iron, your fields of fruit and grain;
I love your bloomclad orchards where dwells the honey bee;
I love you, Alabama, you're the only state for me.

**Chorus:**
O'er many states I've wandered to find the nation's best,
But my heart turns back to Dixie, Alabama, here we rest;
Where majestic Lookout mountain keeps his watch o'er all below,
O'er the sun-land where the Coosa and the Alabama flow.

I love your crystal brooklets as they sparkle on their way;
I love your Noccalula falls, I love your Mobile bay;
I love your golden sunsets, your birds sing day and night;
I love the jaunty mocking bird, the whippoorwill and pert bob white;
I love your rain and sunshine, your mines of richest ore;
I love your healthful climate, I love you more and more;
I love your genial people, they're the truest of the true;
I loved you in my childhood and will love you till I'm through.

*Published by Z.T. Spencer, Gadsden, Alabama*
*Price 10 cents*            *Copyright, 1915, by Z.T. Spencer*

# *Index*

## ▪ C ▪

# ▪ S ▪

### ▪ T ▪

### ▪ U ▪

### ▪ V ▪

### ▪ W ▪

### ▪ Y ▪

### ▪ Z ▪